FLAVOR QUILTS
For Kids To Make

Complete Instructions for Teaching Children to Dye, Decorate & Sew Quilts

Library of Congress Cataloging-in-Publication Data

Amor, Jennifer.
Flavor quilts for kids to make: complete instructions for teaching children to dye,
decorate and sew quilts / Jennifer Amor.
p. cm.
ISBN 0-89145-987-1: $12.95
1. Patchwork.   2. Textile painting.   3. Dyes and dyeing – Textile fibers.   I. Title.
TT835.A485   1991
746.9'7 dc20

91-43200
CIP

Additional copies of this book may be ordered from:

American Quilter's Society
P.O. Box 3290
Paducah, KY 42002-3290

@$12.95. Add $1.00 for postage & handling.

Copyright: 1991 Jennifer Amor

Printed by IMAGE GRAPHICS, INC., Paducah, Kentucky

FLAVOR QUILTS
For Kids To Make

Complete Instructions for Teaching Children
to Dye, Decorate & Sew Quilts

JENNIFER AMOR

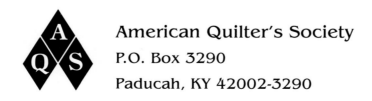

American Quilter's Society
P.O. Box 3290
Paducah, KY 42002-3290

DEDICATION

This book is dedicated to John, Michelle and Jonathan,

who learned to survive while I was on the road,

and to all the wonderful teachers, administrators, children and

volunteers who have made the Flavor Quilt

such an interesting adventure.

Table of Contents

I.   How To Use This Book   6

II.   The Flavor Quilt Project   7
How the Flavor Quilt Project was invented

III.   Working With Children   9
Helpful hints, do's and don'ts, making family, party,
neighborhood, club, school and church quilts

IV.   Dyeing With Powdered Soft Drink Mix   13

V.   Decorating Fabric With Crayons   17

VI.   Dye Sticks   22

VII.   Fabric Paints   24

VIII.   Rubber Stamps   34

IX.   Teaching Children To Sew   37
Tips for simple hand sewing with children of all ages

X.   A Quick Basic Quilting Course   44
Timesaving tricks: rotary cutters, strips, machine sewing
and other helpful hints

XI.   Making A Miniature Flavor Quilt   56
Complete directions for an 8" square miniature quilt

XII.   The Large Flavor Quilt   61
Complete instructions for a full-sized 82" x 57" quilt, including
preparation, construction, basting, quilting and finishing.

XIII.   The School Quilt Project   87
Setting up a residency, funding, themes and curriculum, lesson plans
and outlines for a week-long residency, a one-day or half-day workshop

XIV.   Quilt Books For Children   96
A treasury of quilt-related reading for children

XV.   Sources & Resources   98

How To Use This Book

Who can use this book?

Parents, grandparents; teachers, club leaders, youth workers; neighbors, friends, relatives.

Writing a quilt instruction book for many different audiences is a challenging task. If too little information is provided, a non-sewer may easily become lost. If too much basic information is offered, an experienced quilter may easily become bored. How to compromise?

This book has been divided into sections so that each chapter is a fairly self-contained unit. Though primarily designed for use by adults working with children, many of the techniques can also be used by adults working alone, or with other adults.

All of the chapters on dyeing and surface design can be applied to many other textile projects, and not just quiltmaking.

The basic quilting course chapter covers only the bare necessities. There are dozens of good beginner quilting books on the market, and many quilt shops and guilds offer classes. The techniques mentioned provide a non-traditional approach to quiltmaking using modern gadgets and timesaving tricks. This chapter is aimed primarily at school teachers, club leaders and non-sewers. Experienced quiltmakers may be able to skim through this chapter, or skip it altogether!

The Miniature Quilt project makes a good "trial run" before tackling the full-sized quilt. The techniques of surface decoration and construction are the same for both. This is also a good one-day workshop project and a group project which allows the children to keep their work.

The Large Quilt chapter includes instructions for many different aspects of quiltmaking, from cutting the fabric through basting and machine quilting. It pulls all the information in the previous chapters together into a single project. Before making a large quilt, the reader must first study all the previous chapters.

Teachers interested in making a large school quilt will find a chapter devoted to such topics as funding, lesson plans, themes that can be integrated into the curriculum, and outlines for several different types of workshops.

The final chapters include lists of suggested reading books for both children and adults, and supply sources for some of the products used.

Who can use this book?

Anyone who likes to try something new, anyone who likes to have fun, anyone who is creative, anyone who enjoys spending time with children – anyone!

The Flavor Quilt Project

"How on earth did you come up with this idea?"

It's a question I'm often asked. The "How" is fairly simple; "Why?" is what I frequently ask myself on rainy winter mornings when I'm facing hours of driving in the dark to arrive by 7:30 a.m. at my first class, fresh and enthusiastic!

So how did an unemployed journalist find herself driving 45,000 miles in four years, teaching thousands of children to make quilts?

In 1985, my journalist husband was promoted and moved to Columbia, South Carolina, by his paper. I left behind a house and a city that I loved, a super quilt guild, a network of creative and inspiring friends, and a growing career teaching adult quilting classes. People were taking notice of my bargello quilts, my intricate Graphed Strip Piecing technique, and my machine cutwork and applique.

It took several years to rebuild that network with new friends, a new guild. While I struggled to establish new adult classes, I learned about the Artists in Education program administered by the South Carolina Arts Commission.

This nationwide program, sponsored in part by the National Endowment for the Arts, places professional artists in schools and community organizations for anything from one day to 32 weeks.

The program is a unique interaction with visual, literary, media and performing artists. It is designed to awaken and reinforce the natural creativity of participants, build art audiences for the future, and enrich everyday experience.

In South Carolina and many other states, professional artists must first have their work juried by the Arts Commission, or meet a series of established criteria. The current directory of "approved" artists in this state is over an inch thick, with people from many other states – including dancers, musicians, potters, puppeteers, painters and papermakers.

Each year, the Arts Commission holds a "hiring conference" which brings together the artists and representatives of schools and community organizations who have applied for matching grants to fund programs in their area. In small, rural areas there may be money for only one visiting artist per year; in larger metropolitan areas there may be dozens of residencies.

Once I was approved to work, the next step was to get myself hired. There were moments of sheer panic, thinking about making quilts with children. I knew I had to come up with a gimmick, something different and catchy.

I had taken classes in silk painting and gradation dyeing. I'd made "handprint" aprons in my preschooler's class. I'd played with fabric crayons. The idea started to form.

I knew commercial dyes were too dangerous and expensive to use with small children, but the "big flash" didn't come until a friend made a joke about a red powdered soft drink mix.

On a sunny winter afternoon, I grabbed my preschooler and his playmate, took hot water, packages of drink mix, fabric, paint and crayons into the garden. By the end of the day I had learned a lot, and the Flavor Quilt was born!

The night before that first hiring conference I couldn't sleep. Would anyone really PAY me to do this? The night after the conference I couldn't sleep. I'd been hired on the spot and now I had to deliver! Terrified, I realized I knew nothing at all about working in schools!

Those first few bumbling residencies took years off my life and taught me what I could – and could not – do. Thousands of students later, I know exactly what works, precisely what to expect, and how to get what I want. The Flavor Quilt has become a thriving business, with more offers of work than I can possibly handle.

When friends and associates in the "grown-up" quilting world learned about my "other life" they bombarded me with questions. While I struggled to make a name for myself on the national quilting scene as a serious designer and teacher, my "flavor quilts" fame spread like crazy. "Forget about the bargello," people said: "Tell us what you're doing with kids."

An article about Flavor Quilts that I wrote for *American Quilter* magazine (Spring, 1990) brought a flood of letters and phone calls from all over the country. Everyone wanted to know how they could do a similar project with children in their area.

I hope this book will answer all those questions. I hope Flavor Quilts will bring the joy of new discoveries to children everywhere. I hope the book will inspire parents, grandparents, Scout leaders, youth group leaders, school teachers and anyone else with a love of "making things" to stitch magical quilts filled with unforgettable memories – joining the threads of the past to the fabric of the future.

When we move again, I'll miss the thousands of friendly people I've worked with in South Carolina. But this time there will be a welcoming committee: new friends in new schools. The Flavor Quilt is ready to hit the road nationwide!

Working With Children

Author and teacher Hiam Ginott wrote: "Concerning a teacher's influence: I have come to the frightening conclusion that I am the decisive element in the classroom. It's my personal approach that creates the climate. It's my daily mood that makes the weather. As a teacher, I possess a tremendous power to make a child's life miserable or joyous. I can be a tool of torture or an instrument of inspiration. I can humiliate or humor, hurt or heal. In all situations, it is my response that decides whether a crisis will be escalated or de-escalated, and a child humanized or dehumanized."

Wise words to remember when working with children, whether you are school teacher, club leader, parent or friend. No matter what your official title or position, when you "make something" with a child, you are the "teacher." Under your leadership, the child can learn to enjoy the task, or to hate it. It's all a matter of approach.

Always keep in mind that the project should be fun! When it stops being fun, put the work away for another time.

Don't underestimate what children can do. Adults – even teachers – are often skeptical of children's abilities. When I deliver a finished Flavor Quilt to a school, children and adults are usually amazed by how good it looks.

With meticulous organization, preparation, and plenty of adult help, any group of children can produce a wonderful quilt.

Here are some points to remember:

- Any age child can create artwork for use in a quilt. Adult help will be needed to transfer that work successfully to cloth (ironing crayon drawings, outlining designs, making handprints).

- Resist the urge to "correct" young children's artwork or to draw an outline for them. Their unique vision of the world may produce charming and unusual images – dinosaurs that look like dogs, odd-shaped humans, houses that would be impossible to build – but they will never draw this way again. All too soon, their wildly original artwork will look just the way it's supposed to. It's much more fun to save those early efforts. You'll cherish them when the children are grown.

- Even preschoolers can sew quilt blocks together by hand, but the younger the child, the more adult supervision will be required.

- If you have unlimited time for your project, older children can cut and mark their own fabric squares. However, in a one-week project, all fabric should be pre-cut and marked. Even high school seniors (and some adults, too) have difficulty marking accurate quarter-inch seams on cloth.

- Accurate construction is vital to the quality of the finished quilt. While children can easily sew the blocks together and join them into rows, every seam should be checked for accuracy during the construction process. Loose seams should be restitched by hand or machine. Be sure to re-cut completed blocks to the correct size before joining them together.

- Work sessions should be geared to the age of the children involved. A 45-minute period may not be enough time for a teenager, but it may be far too long for a preschooler. Very young children often finish their artwork quickly; teen-agers may need much longer to create detailed blocks. The reverse is usually true when it comes to sewing.

- Don't be sexist! Boys often sew much better than girls. Quiltmaking is not "women's work." One of my favorite quilts was made – after much macho groaning – by a high school wrestling team. The table talk was of weightlifting and working out, but the finished blocks were dynamic red and black lightning bolts!

- Volunteers are essential to a successful project. Two adults can handle a group of 25 children during the art portion (four adults for preschool and kindergarten). During the sewing segment you will need one adult for every two or three young children. For grades two through six, one adult for every five children works well. Older children can usually help each other. A major problem for a child is a simple matter for an adult. Nothing is more frustrating for a child than having to wait endlessly for help. Be sure help is immediately available during the sewing portion, or you may have busy fingers being destructive with scissors and needles!

- Be creative when looking for volunteers! If you are doing a school quilt, you may find that most mothers work and cannot help during the day. Try using children from the older grades as helpers. Ask for fathers, grandparents or neighbors. Sometimes other school employees can be pressed into service – bus drivers, office personnel, custodians, classroom assistants and student teachers. Post a notice in the public library. Check the local quilt guild, embroiderer's guild or art club. Ask the extension office. Invite volunteers from a senior citizen's complex or club – they make marvelous surrogate grandparents, and can share their quilting memories (and often their old quilts) with the children. You may need to provide transportation for them, and often, schools will invite them to eat lunch in the cafeteria –

it's an enjoyable outing for older people who may be lonely.

- Keep your sense of humor! Quilting is not a deadly serious business – it should be fun! Try to introduce humor whenever appropriate.

- Beware of discipline problems, especially in a school setting. Let the classroom teacher keep discipline while you handle the quilt. Most children think making a quilt is fun – and it sure beats schoolwork!

- If a child in a group becomes disruptive, take the time to find out – quietly – what the problem is. Teachers can often identify children with terrible home problems, children who are on behavior-altering medications, children who are abused or have attention deficit disorders. Don't be too fast to censure these kids. Most of them have had very few successes in their young lives. With patience, creativity and a little extra effort on your part, you can show them a better way.

Children who perform poorly academically may surprise you by being wonderful artists, or amazingly good stitchers. You can really boost their self-esteem by praising their work (or good behavior) in front of the group.

When a problem student has produced a particularly good picture, or sewn an especially good seam, one of my favorite tricks is to send both student and work to the teacher, or even to the principal. Most of these kids spend a lot of time in the office, being disciplined. It's a rare joy to go there for praise and congratulations for doing a good job. Very often, these are the children who will beg you not to leave at the end of the project. You know then that you've made a difference in their lives.

SOME IDEAS FOR MAKING QUILTS

For hundreds of years, children's quilts have been carefully sewn by loving mothers and grandmothers. Precious memories have been handed down by one generation to the next. Children's quilts have been so constantly used and washed and used again that very few really old examples still exist. Those that do are highly prized – and priced – by collectors.

Quilts made by children, however, are a completely different species. A small child's artwork and chubby handprints on a wallhanging may not be worth much on the open market, but to that child's family, those scraps of cloth are a priceless heirloom. Today's adults are rediscovering the joys of fine handcrafting, but how many are passing along those skills to children?

Children's quilts can be as small as a single block made by one child (see Chapter 11), or as ambitious as a large wallhanging suitable for a group of 100 children (see Chapter 12).

Use your imagination to design the basic quilt size and shape to suit your needs. It's not necessary to make pieced quilt blocks for your quilt. If time is short, simply have people make large fabric crayon drawings which can be ironed onto blocks of fabric later – no need to sew dozens of little pieces together! Handprints or autographs can be made directly on large fabric squares, or on long border strips. Choose a bright print to use as lattice or sashing when you join your large blocks into a quilt.

Here are some other ideas for making group quilts:

THE FAMILY QUILT – Take your quilting supplies to a family gathering and have every family member design a block. Use autographed family handprints—or footprints—for blocks or borders. The entire family can sew the quilt, or one member can stitch it. Be prepared to make extras! Everyone will want one when they see the finished quilt.

If your family lives all over the place, mail paper and fabric crayons to different members, collect all the designs and make the quilt yourself. A small family could make blocks of favorite events, pets, houses, or vacations. A quilt makes a great surprise gift for grandparents or a wedding anniversary.

THE COUSINS QUILT – A variation on the family quilt, this one involves only the cousins (or brothers and sisters). My brother and I both have sons the same age. Once a year, when they visit, we make two sets of handprints and a series of fabric crayon drawings. All the artwork is signed and dated. The handprints have changed from small and chubby to large and skinny over the years. Soon I'll have enough blocks to make two quilts – one for each cousin.

THE FRIENDS' QUILT – Another variation on the family/cousins quilt, this time using a child's friends. Gather all the kids in the neighborhood, or invite all your child's friends for a quilting party. If you're not up for a large group, have your child's friends make drawings and handprint blocks when they come over to play. It only takes a short time, and when you collect enough, you can make a quilt. What a great "memory" quilt for a child who is moving to another town.

THE BIRTHDAY PARTY QUILT – Have each guest make autographed designs and handprints for quilt blocks. Sew the blocks into a wallhanging with bright party-type fabric in the lattice or sashing. Be sure that a block identifies the birthday child and the date.

THE CELEBRATION QUILT – This is the same as the birthday quilt, with party guests of all ages making the blocks and handprints for a quilt to celebrate a baby shower, wedding shower, anniversary party, Christmas or Easter party, or any other type of special occasion. Finish off the blocks with fabric appropriate for the occasion. Be sure everyone signs the quilt, and make a special block telling when the quilt was made, and the occasion it celebrates.

THE NEIGHBORHOOD QUILT – The same as a family quilt, but use your neighbors and their families. Have an outdoor picnic or block party and invite everyone to make a quilt block. A good fund-raiser for a neighborhood association (raffle the finished quilt), or a gift for a special person.

THE TEACHER QUILT – What better way to thank a terrific teacher than to have "her kids" make a secret quilt! With a small class, such as a preschool class, choose a time when the teacher will be away – or ask the administrator to arrange for her absence – so you can accomplish most of the artwork during school time. If this isn't possible, circulate crayons and paper through the car pool, and have one after-school session to do handprints. A committee of mothers could construct the quilt. Perhaps each mother could quilt her own child's block. Start the project several months before the end of school, so the finished quilt can be presented on the last day.

THE CLUB/SUNDAY SCHOOL/SCOUT/ WHATEVER QUILT – No matter what type of organization your child belongs to, individual miniature quilts can be sewn, or a group quilt can be made as a special gift for a leader, as a fund-raiser to raffle off, or simply as a learning experience. In many adult quilt groups, members work on a Friendship Quilt each year. Everyone makes a block, or helps with the quilting, keeping track of the number of hours worked. When the quilt is finished, chances are given according to the number of hours each person donated. Names are drawn at the annual holiday party or a meeting, and the lucky winner keeps the quilt!

Use your imagination and you won't need an excuse to start a quilt with your child! The time spent together, working, will build very special memories for you both.

Young children like to have something to show for their labor. Hanging a child's finished quilt in a place of honor, or carefully wrapping it as a gift for Grandma, builds confidence and self-esteem. Children need to know that their work has worth. You can demonstrate this to them by treating their creations with respect. Later, when your kids are grown, their early quilting efforts will be some of your priceless treasures.

Working in groups is also a good experience. You're not just making a quilt, you're building a sense of community, a coming together of children and adults.

Much more goes on during this project than just quilting. In addition to the art, the math, the history and the social studies, children learn how to share, how to work as a group, how to perform under pressure. They learn about quilts in their family, who made them, and why.

Call the local newspaper or television station and ask for coverage of your project. Enter your finished work in a quilt show, or hang it in a library or museum.

One teacher in a rural area took her quilt and several students to the State House. Hundreds of politicians, lawyers and business people admired the children's work.

Often, a school quilt will be featured in the local newspaper or on television. Several group quilts have won blue ribbons at regional quilt shows. These experiences teach children that their art is important, that they can make things with their own hands. It's a huge boost to small egos.

Working with children takes a lot of energy and a good sense of humor, but the end results are worth all the effort. You'll learn a great deal from them – they will really expand your world.

Whether you are a paid professional, or an unpaid volunteer, the children's hugs and parents' congratulations will give you a wonderful cozy feeling – just as if that quilt you've helped to make has wrapped itself around your heart.

Dyeing With Powdered Soft Drink Mix

"Is it permanent? How do you wash it?"

Always the first question, this is a tough one to answer. Yes, the powdered soft drink mix is fairly permanent – have you ever tried to remove the red kind from clothes or carpets? How do you wash it? Since the quilt is designed as a wallhanging, and not as a bed covering, it's tempting to say you wash it the same way you wash a watercolor painting!

This is really a case of art versus craft: nobody asks how to clean a painting when they buy it, because a painting, as everyone knows, is meant to hang on a wall. A quilt, however, is too often viewed merely as "craft," and therefore must have a function – so if you use it, you must clean it!

The dye in powdered soft drink mixes is not wash-proof, and it will fade when exposed to strong light, the same as any other dye. If you follow the dyeing directions carefully, and look after the finished quilt, you can expect to have many years' enjoyment from the packaged drink mix colors. Processed fabric can be rinsed very lightly in cold water, but there will be some dye loss. The best way to preserve it is not to let it get wet at all. Regular shaking or vacuuming will remove surface dust.

Another frequently-asked question: "Isn't it awfully sticky?" can also be answered quickly. "The fabric doesn't care what it tastes like!" You don't need sugar to dye fabric!

FABRIC – THE MOST IMPORTANT "SECRET INGREDIENT"

The single most important factor in dyeing with powdered soft drink mix is the type of fabric you use. Although the process will work with the unbleached muslin you can buy in your local fabric store, the best results and the deepest color can be obtained only with completely natural, untreated fibers, such as unmercerized, non-permanent press, unbleached 100% cotton muslin. This is the kind of fabric fiber artists use for dyeing. Both the mercerizing and the permanent press process add chemicals to the fabric that prevent the bonding of dye molecules with the fibers. The same is true with synthetic fibers – the food dye in the drink mix is simply not strong enough to remain in the fabric. Your colors will be very pale, and, except for red, will wash out easily.

Weavers use powdered drink mix to dye natural fibers such as wool, linen and silk. It can also be used to dye handmade paper.

Check the Sources & Resources section of this book if you cannot find suitable fabric in your area. You may be able to obtain unmercerized muslin from an upholstery store, since this kind of inexpensive cotton is sometimes used "inside" furniture before the outer layer of fabric is attached.

As with all dyeing and painting of textiles, the fabric should first be washed to remove the sizing. Washing in hot water alone is best. Do not use bleach or fabric softener. If you use a detergent, be careful that it does not contain a built-in softener, as this will leave a film on the fabric that repels the dye.

Remember that untreated cotton fabric shrinks a good deal and also wrinkles horribly. Anything longer than two or three yard pieces will be difficult to handle. The best way to deal with it is to smooth the wet fabric, then air dry until it is damp. Iron immediately, while damp, with a very hot steam iron. You can roll the damp fabric tightly and store in a sealed plastic bag in your refrigerator for several days, if necessary. Be careful not to leave it too long, or the fabric will mold and mildew. If you're really busy, you can freeze the fabric until you have time to iron it! For large projects, ask your fabric store for their discarded cardboard bolt boards, and keep the ironed muslin wrapped around a board so it won't wrinkle.

GETTING READY TO DYE

If you're working with a small group of children, the best place to dye fabric is outdoors, on a warm, dry, sunny day. The solar heat helps fix the dyes in the fabric, and the whole process can be accomplished in several hours with very little mess.

Indoors, or in the classroom, allow several days to achieve the best color. The longer you leave the fabric in the dye bath, the more intense the color will be. Allow at least 48 hours.

There are several brands of powdered soft drink mixes on the market. You may have to experiment with the brands available to you to find those that give the most intense color. Some brands may require more packages to achieve the strongest colors.

The quantities given are for dyeing twenty to thirty 3" squares. You may double the recipe for a larger batch, or decrease it for a smaller amount (one package to ¾ cup water is a good formula). The dyeing process remains the same, regardless of the batch size.

Since the process requires boiling water, an adult should supervise children. If you have never made a quilt before,

read the chapter in this book on basic cutting and marking techniques before you dye the fabric.

MATERIALS AND EQUIPMENT
- 20-30 3" squares prewashed 100% cotton, unbleached, unmercerized, non-permanent press muslin (mark ¼" seam allowances on back of fabric with a pencil)
- 4 pkg. unsweetened powdered soft drink mix (any red flavor, orange, grape or lemon-lime)
- Plastic buckets or bowls
- Stirring spoons or sticks
- Cold rinse water
- Boiling water
- 1 tablespoon salt
- Plastic garbage bags
- Rubber gloves (optional)

METHOD
- Dissolve 4 packages of a single flavor drink mix and salt in a bucket, using about a quart of boiling water. Stir well. (The salt helps to set the dye.)
- Fill a second bucket with cold water. Dip individual fabric squares in this bucket of cold water, squeezing out excess moisture. Let each child be responsible for one or more squares.
- Drop wet fabric squares into hot drink mix, stir well and allow to soak. The longer you leave the fabric in the dye bath, the deeper the color will be. A few squares can be dyed in a solution of one package to ¾ cup boiling water in a matter of hours, especially if you use the hot sun to keep the solution warm. Larger batches should be left overnight or up to 48 hours. (The dye bath will mold if left too long.) Stir dye bath occasionally, making sure all fabric is under the surface. Do not mix flavors, unless you want to create new colors – usually brown.

NOTE: If you are working with a group in a

one-day project, process a batch of fabric beforehand. Allow participants to dip and dye fabric in the workshop, then take the buckets home, process them yourself and use them for the next project.

- When fabric has achieved a nice, deep color, squeeze out excess drink mix, gently smooth fabric squares onto a garbage bag that has been taped to a flat surface, and allow cloth to dry. If the fabric remains wrinkled, a marbleized effect is achieved. Squares that are the same color can touch, but different flavors will bleed together to form new colors. The drink mix dye will mark clothing (the reds are especially permanent) and stain hands for several days. Try using rubber gloves. Be sure to wash hands between flavors to avoid mixing dyes. Fabric will dry faster outdoors, but avoid direct sunlight and watch out for windy days. Try anchoring the garbage bags with stones, or tape them to a picnic table.

- When the fabric has dried completely, put about 2 cups of cold water in a bucket and working with one color at a time, drop dyed fabric in and swish around lightly. If you rinse too heartily, you'll remove most of the dye! Just drop fabric in, stir a few times and squeeze out. Change rinse water for each flavor.

- Smooth rinsed fabric back onto garbage bags, being careful to put the reds back on the red bag, greens on the green bag, etc. If you forget which is which, clean the bags with a damp paper towel. Allow fabric to dry completely.

- Iron dyed fabric with a very hot steam iron. Trim excess "strings" from the edges.

- Store dyed fabric squares in self-closing plastic sandwich bags until you're ready to sew.

HELPFUL HINTS FOR DRINK MIX DYEING

Kids of all ages love dyeing with powdered drink mix. Teachers often say the school never smelled so good! Although the mixture is non-toxic, it's probably not very clean, judging by the color of the "dip" water bucket! However, there will always be a few kids who just have to taste the dye bath when your back is turned.

I travel with a small electric tea kettle for boiling water. Another time-saver, especially in damp weather, is a small hair dryer. I drop the wet fabric squares, one flavor at a time, into an empty plastic bucket and use the hair dryer on high until the fabric dries. Clean the bucket between colors.

Keep an eye on the dye buckets; somebody always tries to mix the colors. When working on a group project, explain to the kids that they will not get their "own" dyed piece back to sew. I usually have each class dye a different flavor, starting with green, since it takes the longest to set.

Although weavers have obtained good dye results with yellow and blue drink mix flavors on wool, I have had no luck at all with the muslin. All of the red flavors, including the fruit punch mixes, work easily and quickly, and give the most intense color. Green, or lemon-lime, is the hardest color to dye and the easiest to wash out. A lot depends on the chemical composition of the water you use. Green is especially hard to dye in areas near the ocean. If your tap water gives you trouble, try using bottled water.

In the dyebath, colors will appear much darker. After the first drying, the fabric will be stiff and dull. The reds and purple will look brownish. Once the fabric is rinsed, a much nicer color will appear, and the fabric will be soft again, especially after being steam pressed.

Grape usually looks more gray or brown than purple. You can make different colors by mixing a little red with purple or orange. Use less red if you want a pastel pink.

Treat the fabric squares gently when smoothing them out to dry, or squeezing them. The edges will ravel easily, and you can quickly lose your seam allowances.

Stock up on powdered drink mix during the summer. Some stores don't carry as many flavors during the winter.

The dye process described above evolved from four years of experimenting with different techniques. I have tried baking, boiling and microwaving. Baking removed all the finish from my cookie sheets and made them rust. It also fried the fabric. Boiling didn't make much difference to the finished color. Drying in a clothes dryer left enough residue on the dryer drum to turn a batch of wet towels pink. Ironing wet squares dry between paper towels removed a good deal of the color. Wearing rubber gloves saved my hands from days of being stained a nasty green-brown color.

Have the kids do all the work except boiling the water and ironing. With supervision, kids can achieve great results, and they don't mind having strange-colored hands!

Decorating Fabric With Crayons

Crayola® Fabric Colors by Binney & Smith Inc. are ideal for use by small children, but older children and adults can also create challenging and interesting effects with them.

Similar in appearance to the waxy crayons familiar to children of all ages, Crayola® Fabric Colors can be found in fabric, craft and art stores and in the craft departments of many department and discount stores. They come eight to the pack, and though the colors appear drab on paper, they become lovely and bright when ironed onto fabric.

The process is simple: draw a picture on paper with the crayons, then iron the picture onto fabric and it will magically appear on the cloth.

Unlike regular crayons, Crayola® Fabric Colors are made with a permanent fabric dye. When heated with an iron, the dyes release from the paper and bond with the molecules of the fabric.

Because they are so familiar, fabric crayons are extremely easy for children to use. If the child doesn't like the design, the paper can be discarded and the child can begin again. No fabric is wasted. This is especially important when working with large groups.

A WORD ABOUT FABRIC

You MUST use a SYNTHETIC fabric to make the colors permanent. Although fabric crayons transfer nicely to 100% cotton, the colors will fade over time until eventually, all color disappears.

The heat-setting process becomes permanent only with a synthetic fabric. The dye in the crayons is released with heat, and interlocks permanently with the molecules of synthetic fabric. If you use 100% synthetic fabric, you should achieve 100% permanency. If you use a blend of 50% polyester and 50% cotton, about 50% of the color in your fabric will fade away over a period of time. Only the dye that adheres to the synthetic fibers in the blend will remain in the cloth.

Unfortunately, transferring the drawing from paper to fabric requires a very hot or "cotton" setting on your iron. The heat can easily damage synthetic fibers. You will need to experiment with various fabrics to find one that has a high synthetic content (at least 50% or 60%), but is also a heavy enough weave to resist shriveling under the hot iron.

Binney & Smith Inc. suggest 100% synthetic fabrics like polyester knits, gabardine, interfacing, poly-felt, suede-like cloth, acetate or nylon. Since none of these are particularly suited to quiltmaking, you might consider appliqueing the finished synthetic onto cotton.

In my own experimenting, I have found that high polyester fabrics consistently shrivel as much as ¼" on the lengthwise grain for each 3" square tested. At lower iron temperatures, the pictures do not transfer completely. Using a sheet of typing weight paper between the iron and the design minimizes heat damage to the fabric.

When working with a small project, iron drawings onto larger pieces of fabric, and then cut to size. When working with a group project where squares of fabric must be pre-cut and marked, choose your material carefully and add ⅛" to the measurement of your small square to avoid a loss in size.

To obtain bright, true colors, begin with a white fabric. Colored fabrics will change the colors of the crayons. As with all fabrics used in dyeing and painting, prewash to remove sizing, and do not use bleach or fabric softener.

Although cloth decorated with fabric crayons can be machine washed on gentle cycle in warm water, it should never be put in the dryer. The heat from a dryer will reactivate the dye and cause it to transfer again, effectively fading the picture.

MATERIALS AND EQUIPMENT

- Crayola® Fabric Colors (8 colors in the box)
- Paper (typing, lined notebook or copy machine paper works well; construction and heavy drawing paper are too thick to transfer; newsprint and tracing paper tear too easily during coloring). Cut paper to finished size of fabric squares (original size minus the ¼" seams.)
- Pencil with eraser
- Synthetic fabric (white)
- Iron
- Newspaper and white paper for ironing pad

METHOD

- Lightly sketch a design on paper with pencil. Remember, this is a REVERSE printing process: All letters, numbers, maps and other "one way" designs will have to be drawn backwards. To do this, write normally on the back of the paper with a pencil. Turn to the front, hold paper up to the light (a sunny window is good) and trace the reversed letters onto the right side of the paper. Color the right side only. Young children should avoid any design that needs to be reversed.
- Color the design with fabric crayons. Pressing heavily to create a thick, shiny layer will give the brightest colors. For

pastel colors, such as sky, rub lightly on the paper. Colors can be combined to create new shades. Work on a smooth surface. Fill in all areas until no paper shows through. If you want the color white, leave paper blank. When filling in large background areas, it's easier to turn a piece of crayon on its side, using the flat edge to create a smooth look. For fine lines, break a crayon and use the newly-broken edge. Remember that pencil will not transfer to the cloth, so all important pencil lines must be colored in with crayon.

- Brush specks of crayon from front and back of drawing with a paper towel, otherwise these will transfer, too. Color on one side of the paper only. Heat will transfer both pictures if you have drawn in crayon on both sides of the paper. To keep your design clean, use a larger sheet of paper underneath for a "table mat."
- The design is now a dyesheet, ready to be transferred. Protect ironing board or table with a pad of newsprint topped with a sheet of white paper.
- Set iron to "cotton," no steam. Consider covering your steam iron plate with heavy aluminum foil to avoid a vent pattern on the design. This also allows for easy cleanup if material is scorched and sticks to the iron plate. If you plan to do a lot of fabric decoration, invest in a small iron just for crafts. The surface "goop" can be cleaned when cold by rubbing with very fine steel wool. Art supply books sometimes list "dry" irons that have no steam vents, just a flat, smooth surface.
- Place the fabric on the clean sheet of paper on top of the ironing pad. Position dyesheet face down, crayon side on the cloth. Place another sheet of clean paper over the back of the drawing to protect both fabric and iron.

- Press the hot iron slowly over the entire design, being careful not to hold the iron in one spot (you'll get white circles from the steam vents). Use a lifting motion when moving the iron, to avoid blurring the design. The image will become visible on the back of the dyesheet. Keep the iron moving for several seconds, being careful not to move the dyesheet. Carefully lift a corner of the paper to check the transfer.
- When color looks intense and there are no faded areas, remove dyesheet. If you have missed an area, you can carefully re-align the design and iron some more.
- The design can be re-colored and used again on another piece of fabric. Always use a clean area of paper under each design that you iron. The shadowy images that come through the cloth onto the paper will also transfer back into the next piece of fabric.

If you are ironing several designs, the time required for each transfer will decrease as your ironing surface becomes hotter. Be sure to make allowances for this, or you may "fry" your fabric!

NOTE: ALWAYS have an adult do the ironing. The iron, fabric and paper are all extremely hot and there is a danger of burns and potential for fire. Fumes from the wax and paper may bother people with allergies. Have children stand back and watch their faces while you perform the magic!

IDEAS FOR WORKING WITH FABRIC CRAYONS

Crayola® Fabric Colors can be used in various ways to create colorful designs. With the points, you can get thin lines and small areas. With the sides of the crayon, you can lightly shade background area. Crayons can be sharpened. You can even save the "sharpenings" in a paper cup, mix- ing tiny shavings of many colors. Sprinkle these specks over large areas of background fabric, cover with paper and heat set with the iron. This gives a good overall background design, an unexpected creation!

RUBBINGS

Anything with texture can produce an interesting pattern. Lay a thin piece of paper over embossed greeting cards, heavy lace, plastic strawberry baskets, chunks of wood grain, floor tiles, coins, leaves, rope, paper doilies etc. and rub over the paper with the side of a crayon. The image will appear on your paper. You can make the design look neater by carefully cutting it out around the edges before ironing it onto fabric.

LEAF PRINTS

To reproduce the exact texture of a leaf, color a piece of paper all over with solid crayon to make a dyesheet. Flatten a leaf that has good texture, then place it vein side up on the ironing pad. Lay the colored dyesheet, crayon side down, on top of leaf and iron to transfer the dye to the leaf. Now take the leaf, lay it dye side down on fabric, cover with paper and iron again to produce the exact image. Many flat objects that can be ironed will transfer images this way.

CUTOUTS & COLLAGE

If you want a clean edge to your design, cut away the background paper before ironing. You can also create dyesheets by applying solid color to paper, then cutting shapes from the dyesheets. Arrange your cutouts on a second piece of thin paper and, using a very small amount of glue stick, lightly tack the design in place. The entire design can then be ironed onto fabric.

Do not use transparent tape for this, because the plastic and glue will melt. Use only a tiny amount of glue or it will stain the fabric. Choose a very thin piece of background paper for the design. It may take longer for the heat to permeate the double layer of paper and transfer the dye colors into the fabric.

Another way to have fun with scissors is to fold dyesheets and cut into snowflake or paper doll designs. Both the design and the paper that's cut away (positive and negative) can be ironed onto fabric to create images. Use a piece of paper between the dyesheet and the iron to protect fabric in the cutaway areas.

Older children will like the look of echo or "flip out" designs. Fold a dyesheet in half, then cut designs from the edges. Lightly glue the cut dyesheet to thin background paper, replacing the cutouts in their correct position, but leaving some blank background space around each shape. By outlining the small cut shapes with a black crayon, a 3-D effect is achieved when the design is ironed onto fabric.

STENCILS

Cut a stencil out of heavy paper, such as manila, or thick construction or drawing paper. Lay the stencil on the fabric, then lay a dyesheet, crayon side down, over the stencil. Cover with a clean sheet of thin paper and iron all the layers. The dye will adhere to the fabric only in the cutout areas of the stencil, giving a sharp, clear image.

LETTERING

Kids love to write their names and other messages on fabric, but since this is a REVERSE printing process, normal letters will come out backwards on the cloth – a mirror image. An easy way to avoid this is to write with a pencil or dark marking pen on the back of the design paper, then hold the paper up to a light source (working on

a window is easy) and trace over the letters on the design side. When letters have been colored and ironed onto fabric, they will magically appear the right way!

For more formal lettering, such as a dedication block for a quilt, a paper or plastic alphabet stencil can easily be used by turning it over and tracing the letters backwards. Be sure to flip your design over from time to time, to make sure you're spelling the words right!

Some of the most effective dedication blocks made with crayons leave the letters white and color the background. The letters can then be outlined using a black permanent marking pen after the design is transferred to fabric.

OUTLINING

Because of the textured surface of cloth, designs transferred with crayons are often indistinct or a little fuzzy. Children sometimes forget to fill in the details they've drawn with pencil. Since pencil does not transfer from paper to fabric, details like eyes and fingers are often lost. However, the pencil acts as a dye resist on the fabric, and often will show up as white lines.

To "clean up" the design, you can trace over these white lines, or outline images and letters, using an EXTRA FINE POINT PERMANENT black marking pen. Be sure the marker specifies the ink is permanent on fabric. Marking pens can be bought in several colors of ink, but not all colors are washable. Some pens are permanent only on paper, plastic etc. Test the pen on a scrap of fabric to be sure it doesn't bleed, then heat set the ink by ironing it.

Laundry marking pens can be bought with various size points. Many of these tips are quite wide, and bleed easily on fabric. Look for an "Extra Fine" point, rather than a "Fine" or "Medium," and draw with quick, light strokes to avoid bleeding. While many types of stores sell laundry pens, the extra fine points can usually be found only in an art or office supply store.

To outline children's drawings, use one continuous black line, rather than lots of short, feathery lines. Follow the original pencil line to achieve an effect like a coloring book outline. This makes the drawings show up beautifully, and does not distract the viewer from the child's creation. Resist the temptation to "improve" on the child's artwork! Just follow the pencil lines, using the original paper as a reference.

FABRIC CRAYONS VERSUS REGULAR CRAYONS

Using crayons on fabric is not new. Mothers and teachers have been sewing children's artwork into quilts for years. Many people have told me they used regular crayons, and not the special fabric colors, and achieved perfectly acceptable results.

I have found that regular crayons will not transfer from paper to fabric. Often, in a classroom, regular crayons become mixed in with baskets of fabric crayons. The colors may look much prettier on paper, but alas they will not transfer to fabric.

Ordinary wax crayons must be used directly on fabric. Since it's difficult for children to draw on a surface that wrinkles and moves, the fabric can be taped to cardboard or a hard surface. When the drawing is finished, iron the fabric using waxed paper or regular paper on top of the drawing to protect the iron, burn off the wax, and set the colors into the cloth. According to Binney & Smith's consumer specialists, regular Crayola® crayons are made with pigment, whereas the Crayola® Fabric Colors contain a heat activated dye. When used with synthetic fabric, the dye

bonds permanently and should last as long as the fabric. With regular crayons, that bonding does not occur, though the pigment may melt into the fibers as the wax is burned off by a hot iron.

Another disadvantage to working directly on fabric is that there is no margin for error. If the child makes a mistake, or doesn't like the design, the fabric is ruined. It's a lot easier to throw away paper and start again!

If you must work directly on fabric, why not use dye sticks instead of crayons? The next chapter explores this alternative.

STORING FABRIC CRAYONS

If you've ever left a pack of wax crayons in your car on a hot summer day you know they melt easily. Fabric crayons melt at a much lower temperature than regular crayons, and have one other alarming capability: when they melt into upholstery, the colors become permanent! Never leave fabric crayons in a hot, sunny car. At home or in the classroom, store fabric crayons in a cool location.

Dye Sticks

If you're looking for the permanency and intensity of paint combined with the convenience of a crayon, then dye sticks are the way to go!

But be warned: dye sticks are difficult for young children to use properly. Unless you can give constant supervision and assistance, save dye sticks for older children and adults.

Pentel® FabricFun™ pastel dye sticks come in boxes of 15 vivid colors. You can usually find them at art and craft stores, or your school art teacher can order them from art suppliers.

The dye sticks look just like oil pastels – soft, creamy sticks wrapped in paper – and have a much broader color range than fabric crayons. Because they're so soft, young children invariably crush them very quickly. Heat from little hands tends to melt the sticks, too.

The dye sticks are applied directly to fabric. Most children press too hard and apply far too much color to the fabric. After heat-setting, the fabric will become hard and papery if too much dye stick has been used.

Because dye sticks are used directly on fabric, there is little margin for error. However, since the dyes do not become permanent until they're ironed, mistakes can be washed out of fabric. Dye sticks will not transfer from paper to fabric.

Dye sticks can be used on prewashed natural fibers such as cotton, silk and wool, all of which can withstand the high temperatures required to permanently heat-set the dyes into the fabrics. Although 100% synthetic fabrics are not recommended by the maker (because they melt at high temperatures), blends can be used if care is taken with the iron.

Be sure to keep your hands clean while you work. Colors smudge easily. Do not press hard!

MATERIALS AND EQUIPMENT
- Pentel® FabricFun™ pastel dye sticks
- Prewashed white or light colored cotton, silk or wool, or polyester/cotton blends
- Cardboard, pins or tape, or freezer paper
- Pencil
- Tissues or paper towels to clean hands
- Newsprint and clean white paper for ironing pad
- Iron

METHOD
- Wash the fabric to remove sizing. All starch must be removed so the colors can be absorbed by the fibers and become permanent. Dry material and iron it to produce a smooth surface.
- Stretch the fabric and pin to cardboard, or tape to a hard, smooth surface. A quick way to immobilize the fabric is to iron it onto a piece of heavy freezer paper. Place the shiny side of the freezer paper against the wrong side of the fabric and briefly iron the dull side of the paper until it sticks to the cloth. The freezer paper can be peeled off and used several times before it ceases to stick.
- Work out your design lightly with a pencil. It helps to sketch on paper first, and then trace your idea onto the fabric using a light source (such as a sunny window) behind the fabric. Another way to work is to trace your design in dark pen on the dull side of the freezer paper before it is

applied to the fabric. Remember, though, the design will be reversed with this method. Trace the design by holding the fabric and freezer paper up to a sunny window.

- Apply dye sticks to the fabric with even strokes in one direction only, to assure a smooth, unbroken layer of color. Unlike when using the fabric crayons, *do not press hard!* Various shadings can be achieved by blending colors together with a fingertip. Dye sticks do not come with sharpened points, but the edge of the stick can be used for thin lines. If a point is needed, carefully shave the dye stick with a knife.

- When the design is finished, cover it with a sheet of paper, or paper towel, and iron it at a very hot setting, no steam. Move the iron around, but not the paper, as you may smudge your design. Be careful not to burn the fabric around the edges of the paper. Avoid breathing the vapor, especially if you have allergies. Make small children stand back from the ironing area. Only adults should use the iron. Check to see that your design is properly set. If color rubs off on your fingers, you have not ironed long enough.

Once the design has been properly heat set, it is completely washable. Colors will stay bright and can be washed in warm water, but do not use a dryer, to be on the safe side.

Remember, the dye sticks are a direct image process; what you draw on the fabric is what you get when you're through. You do not need to draw letters and numbers backwards, as with the fabric crayons.

STENCILS

You can use precut stencils to create designs with dye sticks, or make your own stencils. To make a stencil, draw a simple design on paper. Tape a sheet of clear plastic (acetate) over the design. Lay the two sheets on heavy cardboard or another surface that can't be damaged, then use a craft knife to cut around the design.

You can also make a stencil from construction paper sandwiched between layers of Con-Tact® paper.

Sharpen the dye sticks to get a good, crisp edge on the design, then color through the stencil with even strokes in one direction only. Heat-set the design as before, then use soft tissue to clean the stencil.

Complicated designs with dye sticks should be done using a stencil. Remember not to press hard. Dye sticks are good to use for lettering. As with crayons, you can use an extra fine point permanent marking pen to outline your design.

Fabric Paints

Painting on fabric offers endless possibilities, from the simplest handprint to the most elaborate artwork. It's fun, it's messy, and best of all, it's easy!

With the popularity of painted sweatshirts and T-shirts, even discount stores now carry a wide variety of fabric paints including metallics, fluorescents, glitter and textured or "puff" paints. They come in an astonishing array of spray cans, small jars, squeeze bottles, tubes or pens, and most are dimensional paints that stick to the surface of the fabric, rather than bonding with the fibers. Many will change the texture of the fabric from soft to hard.

While these are fine for use on clothing, there is a whole world of water-based fabric paints available from several makers and sold through art supply stores. Brands include Versatex®, Createx®, Deka® and many others. They are all "textile" or "permanent fabric" paints, and all must be heat set to make them washable.

The color range is unlimited, since colors can be mixed. There are opaques for covering dark colored fabric; metallics and pearlescents to give added sparkle and fluorescents that glow under black light! A colorless extender can be mixed in to create pastel shades.

The paints are water-based, nontoxic, non-stiffening, machine washable and dry cleanable. When properly heat-set, the colors are non-fading, so those chubby baby handprints will still be visible when the child is an adult.

Paints come in tiny jars for small projects, but can also be bought in larger sizes, right up to gallons, for group projects. I usually buy the 8 fluid ounce size of red, blue and yellow for a group quilt. The larger sizes are more economical.

The paint has the consistency of runny ketchup, and is a little thick for stamping and printing. Add a small amount of water to thin it slightly, no more than 15% to 25%. Don't use too much paint, or the excess will peel off the fabric. The texture of the fabric should easily show through the paint.

Although these fabric paints are not toxic, small children must be closely supervised, because spills and splashes cannot be removed from clothing, shoes, wood floors, etc. Always wear a waterproof apron (cut neck and arm holes in a garbage bag for a quick cover-up), and protect floors and table tops with layers of newspaper. A sheet of heavy plastic is the best way to protect your workspace. The plastic should be kept clean with a wet paper towel to avoid getting paint on fresh fabric.

Spills and splashes on clothing, however, will never come out – even though they haven't been heat-set. The paint washes off skin, though blue may take several scrub sessions. Be sure to wash your hands in the bottom of the sink, because even watered-down splashes won't come out of clothing!

To control the mess, work outdoors, but protect decks and patios; they'll stain.

BASIC MATERIALS AND EQUIPMENT
- Prewashed fabric, either cotton or cotton/polyester blend (wash to remove sizing; don't use fabric softener)
- Permanent fabric paint in several colors; include colorless extender for pastel shades

- Newspaper, roll of heavy plastic (from the hardware store) or an old vinyl tablecloth, masking tape, old towel
- Buckets of water, soap, paper towels, garbage can
- Rubber gloves, waterproof apron, old clothes
- Styrofoam meat or produce trays for mixing colors
- Disposable plastic plates or aluminum pie plates
- Circles of ½" thick foam rubber or sponge to fit plates
- Spray bottle of water to dilute paint
- Variety of "gadgets" to use as printing tools (bottle tops, sponges, coins, forks, small toys, leaves, feathers etc.)
- Paint brushes, both bristle and foam; small paint roller; old toothbrushes; small containers of water to clean brushes
- Permanent marking pens
- Iron

SETTING UP YOUR WORKSPACE

Set up a painting area where you have lots of space and easy access to a sink. Protect floors with paper or plastic, taped down to avoid accidents. It's easier to work standing up, so remove all chairs, and cover a large table with layers of newspaper. Top this with heavy plastic. Place several buckets of water and paper towels on the table, along with a large garbage can close by for waste.

I have found that children make less mess when the paint is poured onto a sponge surface, rather like a large stamp pad. Cut ½" thick foam rubber or sponge to fit plastic plates. (The plates that come with microwave dinners are great, because they have high rims – and they're free! Aluminum pie plates are good, too.) Don't use the kind of sponges that have big patterns or "bubble" holes on the surface – these

will leave their impression on your prints. Use a fine-textured foam rubber to get good, even prints.

Shake the paint bottle, then drizzle a small amount of fabric paint over the sponge, like pouring syrup on waffles. Using a spray bottle of water, spritz the sponge several times to get the right paint consistency. Don't make the paint too wet or it will bleed on the fabric. Let the sponge sit for 15 or 30 minutes to allow the paint to soak in.

Set out "gadgets" to print with. These should be washed in the water buckets between colors, then dried before using again. When I work with a group, I keep the "gadgets" in plastic baskets. At the end of the class, the whole basket of tools can be dumped in a bucket or sink, washed, drained and stored.

Keep plenty of paper towels on hand for clean-ups and "test patterns." Keep the work surface clean of paint by washing the plastic, or replacing the newspaper.

GENERAL DIRECTIONS

- Wear old clothes or a waterproof apron. Fabric paint can easily soak through a work shirt and stain good clothing.
- Lay fabric on plastic surface. For large projects, make a pad of newspapers topped with an old towel and covered with plastic. Tape pad to surface, then tape fabric to plastic to hold it smooth.
- Prepare a "paint sponge" (see above), or use a styrofoam meat tray as a palette.
- Dip the object to be printed lightly in paint and make a "test print" on a paper towel. If you are satisfied with the paint's consistency, dip again and print on fabric. Use just enough paint to achieve the color intensity desired. If you use too much paint, the fabric will dry stiff, and the paint may peel off. You should be able to see the texture of the fabric

through the paint. If your paint has too much water, the design will bleed. If your paint sponge gets too dry, you can revive it by spritzing it with water. Unused paint on a sponge or palette can be stored in the refrigerator for several days in a sealed plastic bag. The sponge will mold if it's not refrigerated. Sponges can be rinsed, dried, and used again for the same color.

• Be careful to keep paint sponges clean by washing gadgets in water buckets before changing colors.

• Mistakes can be partially removed by washing fabric, then ironing dry between paper towels. Permanent fabric paint cannot be completely removed once it is on fabric.

• When your design is completed, allow fabric to dry. Follow manufacturer's directions for heat-setting the dry paint. Often, heat-setting involves ironing the wrong side of the fabric, without steam, at the hottest setting the fabric will bear. Generally, iron for 1 minute at hottest setting, 2 minutes at medium or 4 minutes at a warm setting. Fluorescent colors cannot take high heat. Some fabric paints can be effectively set in a clothes dryer. I have heat-set large projects painted on cotton by air drying overnight, then tumbling on high in the dryer for 45 minutes. There was no loss of color when the fabric was washed in warm water and detergent. However, some fabric paints require more heat than a home dryer provides. Painted fabric should be allowed to cure for one week prior to washing.

HANDPRINTS

For small children, handprints – and even footprints – are the fastest and most endearing way to decorate fabric for a quilt. Be sure to "record" your children's handprints on a regular basis. As your chil-

dren grow, their handprints will change from chubby and cute to long and skinny! Be sure to sign and date each print, using an extra fine point permanent marker pen.

Hand and footprints can be done on individual squares of fabric for a single quilt block, or on long strips for the borders of a larger quilt. Pillows, T-shirts, sweatshirts and aprons are also good for handprint decorations.

For a small project, use both hands on one block. For a group project, use one handprint from each child. Try the primary colors – red, yellow, blue – in progression for a border. Or, for a more uniform look, have all the girls do red, all the boys, blue. How about handprints in the school's official colors?

You can even combine colors to make rainbow hands! Try making a "rainbow" paint sponge by drizzling several stripes of color. Don't make the paint too wet, or it will all bleed together.

I have found a paint sponge is the cleanest and fastest way to do handprints, although paint can also be applied with a brush or small roller. You won't get as true a print with this method, because the brush strokes show, but it's a good way to get striped or multi-colored prints.

Originally, I used a plate full of paint, without a sponge. This was really messy, because the children got too much paint on their hands, which left blobs on the fabric. Also, several children smacked their hands down hard on the paint plate, splashing everyone and everything in range!

Here's the way I do handprints for a large group:

• Read the general directions for fabric painting. Set up a paint table close to a sink. Prepare several plates with paint sponges in different colors, spraying the paint lightly with water to dilute it. Don't make the paint too thick or too watery. Keep a spray bottle of water on the table to "revive" the paint. Keep paper towels handy for cleaning up.

- Get two volunteers to help with younger children. One volunteer sends children to the paint table in pairs. The second volunteer washes painted hands. You do the printing.
- Be sure everyone is wearing a waterproof apron or old clothes. Watch out for drips on shoes!
- Spread out the fabric blocks or border strips on the paint table.
- Hold the child's hand and lightly press onto the paint sponge. Don't press too hard or too often, or the paint will become foamy. You need a light, even coating of paint. Don't smear the hand across the paint sponge, or the handprint will come out with smear lines. Lift the hand and check to see that it's completely covered with paint. If there are bare spots, lightly press down on the sponge again.
- Making sure the child keeps his/her fingers slightly apart, press the hand down on the fabric and count to 10. Make sure the child doesn't wiggle any fingers! Press hard on the hand and keep it still.
- Lift the hand straight up, and pass it immediately to the volunteer hand washer. Make sure hands stay in the bottom of the sink. Even splashes of fabric paint are permanent in clothing!
- While the first child's hands are being washed, repeat the printing process with a second child.
- When the first child's hands are washed and completely dry, have him/her autograph the handprint with an extra fine point permanent pen. Use paper towels to cover previous prints and make sure the child doesn't lean on any wet paint. It's easier to write on the dry background

fabric than on the wet handprint, and easier to write in upper and lower-case letters than in cursive. For a group quilt, be sure to get first and last names. Remember your seam allowances; don't put names too close to the edge of the fabric or they'll be hidden when you sew your quilt together.
- Continue with the handprints until borders are finished. For a large group, handprints can be overlapped slightly. Allow fabric to dry, then heat-set with dry iron (see general directions.)

GADGET PRINTING

Here's a chance for children to be inventive. Raid the kitchen "junk" drawer for interesting objects. One of my most treasured printing "gadgets" is a cheap plastic soap holder, covered with small spikes. When dipped in paint, the soap holder leaves a large area of miniature dots – great for background!

Collect interesting shapes: bottle caps, toothpaste caps, empty thread spools, forks, corks, pieces of styrofoam, buttons, small toys, plastic game pieces, dice, paper clips, coins, rocks – the list is endless.

The process is simple:
- Set up a paint table and paint sponges (see general directions).
- Lightly press gadget onto paint sponge. Keep the paint fairly dry.
- Make a test print on a paper towel.
- Print onto fabric.
- Wash and dry gadget before changing colors.
- Allow paint to dry, then heat-set with a dry iron (see general directions).
- Try repeat printing in horizontal, vertical or diagonal lines. Create interesting designs by overprinting with a second color or shape.

FRUIT, VEGETABLE AND SPONGE PRINTS

One of the easiest ways to get an interesting design is to dip a slice of fruit in paint and then print with it! Try to keep the fruit slice fairly dry before applying paint. Apples, oranges, lemons etc. can be used. Don't press too hard with juicy fruits!

Potato or carrot carvings make good stamps. Slice a potato in half, draw your design on the cut edge, then cut away the background to a depth of ¼ inch. The design doesn't have to be intricate – a simple square, triangle or heart is quite effective. Keep the surface fairly dry and make sure the paint isn't too thick. Practice stamping on a paper towel or scrap fabric.

Carrots can be cut the same way, or simply used to make circle and ovals, depending on the carrot's shape.

Similar shapes can be cut from sponges. A moist sponge is easier to cut than a dry one. When printing, keep the sponge shape as dry as possible, pressing it lightly into the paint, and lightly onto the fabric. Try a test print on paper. If your sponge is too wet, the paint will bleed on fabric, and your shape will be lost. The holes in a sponge make an interesting secondary design.

You can make a checkerboard design with several small square sponge shapes (one for each color). Leave a little background space between prints to keep the colors true, or overlap slightly to create new colors.

I have a large collection of small sponge characters (animals, robots, dinosaurs etc.) that came out of my son's toybox. Originally they were packaged like giant vitamin pills, but when dropped in a bowl of hot water, the outer capsules melted and the compressed colored sponges inside "grew" into various shapes. Check your toyshop for these. You may also find cutout sponge shapes in the craft section of discount and sewing stores. Try the baby department, too – sponge bathtub toys may be useful, though many are rather large.

Be sure to keep the sponge shapes fairly dry when printing; otherwise the shape will become a blob on the fabric.

Follow the general directions for drying and heat-setting designs.

RUBBER STAMPS

Check the section on rubber stamps, but replace the stamp pads with fabric paint on sponges. You can create your own stamps by carving erasers. Don't overlook children's erasers which come in interesting shapes such as robots, bears, hearts, etc.

Be sure to keep your paint fairly dry to get a good impression. A wet stamp will give you a blob on fabric (rinse fabric, iron dry and start again).

For more sophisticated prints, apply several colors of paint to the stamp with a foam brush or a small paintbrush. You can mix shades of paint on a styrofoam meat tray palette. Apply the paint thinly and evenly and print immediately, because it dries quickly on the stamp. Clean stamps in water and dry before using again.

Follow the general directions for heat-setting your designs.

SPLATTER PAINTS

Here's an effective, but messy, technique. Kids love it, but be sure to cover your work surface – and them – with plastic! Rubber gloves are a good idea, too.

Dip an old toothbrush, or short bristled paintbrush, in fabric paint. Get it fairly wet. Pull your index finger (or a wooden popsicle stick) against the bristles to spray or splatter paint onto your fabric. Be sure to give children plenty of workspace so they don't spray someone else's masterpiece by mistake.

To create interesting shapes, lay a paper or sponge shape on top of fabric, then splatter all around it. When you remove the paper or sponge, its shape will appear on the fabric, with a painted background.

Stencils can be treated this way, too. Tape the stencil over your fabric and splatter onto the stencil. Carefully remove the stencil and the cut away parts of the design will appear on the fabric.

If you have a completed design on fabric, but the background looks a little bare, try a light splattering of paint all over the design in a compatible color. Keep your paint fairly dry to create a fine mist of color. It not only fills in the plain background, but also ties the whole piece of fabric together. The same effect can be achieved by using diluted fabric paint in a spray bottle. Spritz color lightly all over your design. Don't soak your fabric. When the paint dries, it will be much lighter and give a soft, misty effect to your fabric, a little like air brushing.

See general directions for drying and heat-setting.

PAINT RUBBINGS

Materials with a raised surface – plastic baskets, heavy lace, rope, rough wood, leaves etc. – can be beautifully reproduced on fabric by taking a rubbing, similar to a rubbing made on paper with pencil or crayon.

Instead of a pencil, you will need a small piece of white felt to use as a rubbing tool. Don't use colored felt – the dye may run. If you're working with several colors, use a separate piece of felt for each one.

- Set up your paint table and paint sponge or palette (see general instructions).
- Place your fabric over the textured surface. You may need to tape your textured surface to the plastic if it is likely to move around.
- Dip the felt applicator into the paint. Keep it fairly dry, but make sure the paint has soaked well into the felt.
- Lightly rub the felt on the fabric until the textured surface shows through.
- You will need to clean your "texture maker" when changing colors.
- You can create larger designs by moving the fabric around on the textured surface.
- Allow paint to dry, then heat-set (see general instructions).

Plastic fruit baskets – the kind strawberries come in – make a checkered pattern. Cut the sides out of the basket and lay them under the fabric. The basket bottoms often have a different pattern from the sides.

Try using vinyl lace table mats or cloths, or even paper doilies. If you're using real lace, remember the fabric paint will color it permanently. Since real lace will soak up paint, you may find interesting color mixes unless you dry the lace between color changes.

Try wrapping thin rope several times around a block of wood. Not only can you use it for rubbings, you can also print with the block if you use cotton rope.

The cut end of a piece of lumber often has amazing texture, following the rings of the tree. Again, be careful of color changes, since the fabric paint will soak into the wood.

Use leaves with very prominent veins (usually on the back of the leaf), and rub lightly over a small area of your fabric. You can also tape several leaves to your plastic surface in a pleasing design, and then rub over the entire surface of your fabric. Evergreen branches make interesting designs.

Use your imagination – flowers, tree bark, floor tiles, coins, watch straps, the bottoms of tennis shoes – anything with a textured surface (even other fabrics) – can be used to take a rubbing. When choosing your texture, just remember that fabric paint will be permanent on many surfaces!

LEAF PRINTS AND OTHER NATURAL WONDERS

You don't need to be an artist to create the most wonderful fabric using leaf prints. Almost any leaf will do, from tiny spring shapes to large fall ones, feathery ferns to dainty dogwoods. Even whole small branches can be used. Feathers, flowers and other natural objects can also be used. I even read of one artist who used a human skeleton to print on bedsheets!

LEAVES

- Set up your workspace (see general directions) with a pad of newspapers covered by an old towel, and finally with heavy plastic taped securely to the table. This forms a soft surface to print on.

- Tape prewashed fabric onto the plastic pad.

- Look for leaves that have interesting shapes and raised veins. Fresh leaves are easier to work with, since dried leaves are very fragile. If the leaf curls too much, try ironing it lightly between two paper towels.

- Shake fabric paint and pour several blobs of compatible colors onto a styrofoam meat tray or palette. Colorless extender, pearlescents and metallics can be added for extra interest.

- Use a narrow sponge brush and a few drops of water to mix colors to the right consistency.

- Lay the leaf, vein side up, on a clean styrofoam tray and apply paint all over its surface. Blending several colors on the leaf is very effective. A light coating of paint is all that's needed – rather like

bread very thinly spread with butter.

- Lay the painted leaf, paint side down, on your fabric. Cover with a second piece of fabric, or a paper towel, and press down hard. Be sure to smooth over all parts of the leaf, including the stem.

- Remove the pressing fabric or paper towel, then lift the leaf off the fabric. You should have a perfect impression!

- Repeat the process with the same leaf, or try a different one, until you have created a pleasing pattern. Use the same colors, or change to different ones. An effective design using the same leaf printed in rows begins with pure colors that are gradually blended together, until finally the leaf is a whole new color, for instance pink and turquoise, blended to create purple.

Each time you print, use a clean paper towel, or move your pressing fabric to a clean area to prevent paint transfer. The pressing cloth will have a faint impression of your leaf. Sometimes your pressing cloth is even prettier than your printed fabric! Instead of paper towels, you can also use sheets of paper which become designer wrapping or note paper when dry!

- Allow your fabric to dry, then heat-set (see general instructions).

FEATHERS

Feathers can be printed in the same way as leaves. Look for fairly small sturdy feathers, two or three inches long. I have found that feathers look more real if you separate some of the barbs. A perfect feather is rather dull, whereas a ragged feather makes a more "feathery" print. The feather can be washed in water between color changes.

Feathers are remarkably resilient and can be used indefinitely. The natural oils on the feather resist the fabric paint. Wash your feather before the paint dries and it will be as good as new!

You can also use a feather like a paint brush. Dip its tip in paint and swirl color across your fabric.

LEAF SPRAYS AND GHOSTLY SHAPES

Small branches of leaves and fern fronds are good for creating background fabric. It's really hard to paint an entire branch of leaves, but if you arrange small branches or bunches of leaves on your fabric, you can use a spray bottle of paint and spritz color all around them.

Try to create a fine mist of paint, similar to air brushing. Thin your fabric paint with 15-25% water, so it will spray through a nozzle. Keep the percentage of paint fairly high, or your design will dry too pale to see.

This is a very messy operation, so be sure to cover everything with plastic. You can set up a paint booth in a large cardboard box draped with plastic. You might want to do this outdoors!

Lay your fabric on plastic, arrange your leaves over the fabric, then spritz paint all over everything. Try not to make the fabric too wet. It helps to have your fabric at a slight angle, so you can hold the spray bottle upright and keep it on "mist" rather than "stream." You can use several spray bottles, each containing a different color of paint.

Allow the paint to dry a little before removing your leaves. You should have white leaf "shadows" on your fabric. If you like, you can rearrange your leaves and spray again with a different color, building up several layers of ghostly impressions.

This same technique can be used with other shapes to create circles (spray around a roll of tape), squares (use your strawberry baskets), stencils (try cutting shapes from styrofoam plates) etc. Even splatter painting with a nailbrush, scrubbing brush or paintbrush can create a simi-

lar effect. Just be sure to protect your surroundings. This technique is messy!

TIE DYE WITH PAINT

Creating tie dye with paint is much easier than working with dyes. The process can be as simple as twisting and dipping a small piece of fabric, or sewing, tying or knotting a larger piece.

The small squares of fabric for a quilt are simple for even a young child to tie dye. Push a finger or pencil into the center of the fabric square to create a point, then twist the point tightly in one direction and hold it in place. The twisted part can then be dipped or rolled in paint or pressed lightly onto a paint sponge. Several colors can be used on the twisted section, but be careful to keep your paint sponges as clean as possible. Start from the bottom of the twist, the part with the most fabric, and work up towards the point.

A cleaner way to work with several colors is to use a brush or small squeeze bottle to apply the paint in bands around the twisted cloth. Don't make the cloth too wet. When the fabric square is opened up, the tie dye pattern should form rings of color separated by rings of plain fabric.

For more complex designs, make several twists in the fabric, each one a different size, and vary your color scheme.

The fabric twists can be held in place by rubber bands, although most small children find it hard to get the band tight enough. You can also use string or heavy thread for tying. Paint won't penetrate where the fabric is tied tightly, and this is what creates your pattern.

If your fabric is large enough, you can tie knots in it and then paint. You can also fold the fabric in accordion pleats.

For really intricate designs, sew a running stitch in circles, lines or zigzags, then draw up your threads to create lots of tiny pleats. The paint will be more intense on the edges of the pleats, fading to very pale or nothing at all inside the pleats.

These same techniques can be used for tie dyeing T-shirts or sweatshirts. Spraying shirts is even easier. Thin your fabric paint with 15-25% water and use spray bottles. Hang your shirt outside and spray stripes of color. Where the stripes bleed together, new color combinations will be created. The pattern will soak through both sides of the shirt. If you want the front and back to look different, be sure to pin cardboard or plastic inside the shirt.

SPINNING PAINT DESIGNS

Remember those neat designs your kids brought home from the fair? A piece of heavy paper mechanically spun around in a deep plastic bowl while you squirted paint at it. The paint splashes created radiating circles of color as the paper rotated.

You can create the same kind of splash with fabric paint on cloth. You'll need a paint spinner machine (available at toy shops and run on batteries). Replace the paper with fabric (you may need to staple, pin or lightly glue the fabric to cardboard to make it stiff enough), and use drops of fabric paint instead of poster paint. Follow the spinner's directions to create your designs. Some toy and craft stores even sell these spinners with fabric paints to create small patches for clothing.

Allow the fabric to dry, then heat-set (see general directions).

PAINTING WITH FABRIC PAINT

With all the wonderful techniques for using fabric paint, it's easy to overlook the fact that you can actually paint with it, too!

Set up your workspace (see general directions), using styrofoam meat trays as a palette. Set out small amounts of several

colors, and keep a water jar close by.

Tape your fabric to the plastic table cover, or stretch it slightly by taping or pinning fabric to a piece of plastic-covered cardboard. If you plan to do a lot of painting, you can make more permanent backings by covering heavy cardboard or foamcore board with self-sticking vinyl shelf covering. The paint will wash off the vinyl when your project is finished.

Use soft artist's brushes and paint as you would on paper. It helps to outline an area with a fine-tipped brush, then fill in the design with a larger brush.

Keep the paint fairly thin on the fabric. Remember, the texture of the fabric should easily show through the paint. You can thin the paint slightly with a water-dipped brush. Many colors can be mixed on your palette. Don't forget to use the colorless extender for pastel shades. You can make lighter colors by adding water, but your design may bleed if it's too wet.

If your fabric is fairly transparent, you can tape a heavily outlined paper design underneath it. Be sure your paper design is outlined in waterproof pen or pencil, so it won't bleed into the fabric. You can also use a light box, or tape your design onto a window and trace it onto the fabric lightly with pencil before painting. Iron-on embroidery designs can be used, too. If you're hard up for inspiration, check children's coloring books.

If abstract art is more to your liking, use miniature paint rollers, sponges or brushes to apply the paint to fabric. Paint and wallpaper stores keep a wonderful textured roller to use on plaster ceilings. It's very stiff and wiry, and it leaves a really interesting pattern on fabric.

Another simple trick is to use masking tape as a "resist." Stick several different widths of tape on your fabric to form abstract checks or diagonal lines. Apply paint all over your fabric with a paint roller. Allow the paint to dry and then remove the tape. You will have white lines wherever the tape covered the fabric.

For a more sophisticated design, re-tape the fabric in different directions and apply a second, darker color over the first. If you begin with a light color, such as yellow, and continue with darker colors each time, you can build up quite complicated patterns.

Taping ripped pieces of paper over your fabric also creates interesting patterns using this same technique.

When you have finished painting, allow the fabric to dry and then heat-set (see general directions).

OTHER TECHNIQUES
FOR SURFACE DESIGN

Public interest in textiles has increased tremendously in the last few years. Many new "how-to" books are on the market that give detailed directions for dyeing fabrics, bleaching fabrics, marbleizing fabrics, transferring photocopies to fabrics, simple silk-screening on fabrics – the list is seemingly endless!

Check your local library, quilt or craft store for new listings. Many of these techniques may be suitable for children to use. Be sure to test them yourself before working with children to make sure the techniques are safe and appropriate for the intended age group, and that the results are worthwhile.

Rubber Stamps

Rubber stamps are fun to use on fabric, especially if you want to do repeat designs on large areas. Many art, gift, toy and stationery stores sell rubber stamps, and several mail order catalogues carry dozens of different designs.

When working on fabric, consider the "rolling" stamps: rubber stamps attached to a small roller with a handle. The design is continuous and can be rolled across the fabric to quickly cover several inches – until your ink runs out!

Many commercial stamp pads can be used with fabrics. Check for refill bottles that say the ink is permanent. You can buy blank stamp pads and bottles of different colored ink at an office supply store. Heat-set the ink with a hot iron.

It's always a good idea to do a "test run" before using a new ink on a quilt. Make several stamp impressions on the fabric you plan to use, allow the ink to dry, heat-set by ironing for several minutes, then set your test aside for several days. After the ink has "cured," wash and dry the fabric swatch and check for bleeding or color loss.

Many fabric and craft stores also carry a line of plastic stamps and small bottles of paint to use for ink.

MAKING YOUR OWN STAMP PADS

You can make your own stamp pads using several thicknesses of fabric, white felt or sponge on a styrofoam plate or plastic dish. Use fabric paint thinned a little with water for your "ink." For a clean impression, don't let your "ink" get too wet.

Using fabric paint means you have a limitless color selection for your stamps. You can also create "rainbow" stamp pads with stripes of paint, or use a foam paint brush to apply paint to areas of the rubber stamp.

Mix metallic colors for stamping, or use opaque fabric paints to print on dark fabric. Gold, silver or copper imprints on shiny black fabric are perfectly elegant! They're great for wearable art projects as well as quilts.

Be sure to wash fabric paint off your rubber stamps after each use. If you allow the paint to dry on the stamp, it will build up, layer upon layer, until your stamp impression becomes fuzzy.

MAKING YOUR OWN STAMPS

Remember potato prints? Cut a potato in half, mark a simple design on the cut surface, then carve out the "stamp" with a knife. Carrots can be used the same way. Even without a carved design, you get interesting oval shapes. Make sure the cut surface is dry before you try to print, and wash it off between colors. A potato can be used many times, and even stored in the refrigerator for use the next day. Supervise children – younger ones will need help with the cutting.

Eraser stamps also make interesting shapes, from simple polka dots created by dipping the pencil-top eraser into ink, all the way to elaborate designs carved into the surface.

Any eraser is fine for simple dip and print techniques. Try using different sides of the eraser to get different shapes.

If you want to carve a design, look for the smooth, white, rubbery erasers found in office supply and art stores. The yellowish art erasers carve easily, but also crumble too easily. Regular pink erasers are too hard to carve. The smooth, rectangular white ones are just right.

Draw the design on the eraser with a fine tip, permanent marker. If you're short on ideas, cut small designs from magazines or wrapping paper. Use a piece of carbon paper between the eraser and the design, then trace over the design with a pencil or ballpoint pen. This will transfer the design to the eraser surface.

Use a sharp craft knife to carve out the design. Everything left on the surface will print. Areas scooped out below the surface will not show. If your design is large, you can continue it on a second eraser, stamping them side by side. You can even mount your eraser designs on small blocks of wood to create formal stamps. If you don't carve too deeply, you can make different designs on opposite sides of the eraser.

If the corners of your stamps show up on the fabric when you print, consider cutting them off with a sharp knife. Often a beautiful stamp design is spoiled when areas of the stamp's base accidentally print on the fabric.

MATERIALS AND EQUIPMENT FOR STAMPING DESIGNS ON FABRIC
- Rubber stamps or potato prints, etc.
- Stamp pad with permanent ink or fabric paint
- Prewashed fabric
- Newspaper to protect work surface
- Bucket of water for cleanup
- Iron and an old sheet to protect ironing board cover

METHOD
- Press stamp onto the stamp pad until stamp surface is evenly covered with ink. If using fabric paint, don't let the stamp surface get too wet. Don't get ink or paint on the stamp's corners or background, or these areas will show up on the fabric.
- Press stamp firmly into fabric and hold for several seconds. Don't move the stamp, or your image will be blurred. Make sure your pressure is even so that the entire design is transferred. When using a rolling rubber stamp, roll in a single line until ink is used. Rolling back and forth over the same area will create a jumble of designs.
- Remove stamp, check for a clear image, and allow the ink or paint to dry. Iron fabric on the wrong side with a hot iron for one minute to heat-set the design and make it permanent. Iron longer at lower heat settings.
- Clean stamp surface by stamping on newspaper or paper towels until all color fades. If using fabric paint, wash stamp in cold water and dry before using again. After long periods of use with fabric paint, a rubbery film adheres to the stamp surface, spoiling the sharp image. Some of the film can be peeled off, but it's easier to wash stamps clean after each use. You can also buy a special chemical solution to clean rubber stamps.

When children are working with different colored stamp pads, set up a "stamp table" covered with layers of newspaper. Encourage children to clean the stamps between colors by stamping on the newspaper, or washing the stamps in a bucket of water. Keep a supply of "re-inkers" handy, otherwise all your stamp pads will soon be a dirty brown color.

USING STAMPS CREATIVELY
Once young children discover the instant gratification of rubber stamps, it's hard to tear them away! Children who may be frustrated by their artistic attempts with

fabric crayons and dye sticks like the immediate results of producing an image that actually LOOKS like something on cloth. Some children only want to play with stamps to decorate their fabric.

Encourage creativity in the use of stamps. Collect different kinds of stamps – animals, alphabets, quilt patterns – and show how to create entire scenes, or messages, or repeat designs. If you stamp an animal in the center of a fabric block, use dye sticks or crayons to fill in the background, or color the animal, add trees, sky etc.

Let children examine the patterns they see on clothing and wallpaper. Then show them how to create repeat designs by stamping in straight lines, or on the diagonal, or in random patterns. Combine a formal rubber stamp with geometric shapes, dots and lines.

When the rubber stamps and ink pads become too confining, move on to work with fabric paints and gadget printing.

Teaching Children To Sew

If they're old enough to hold a needle, they're old enough to learn to sew!

It's fun to watch people's reaction when you tell them children are going to sew a quilt together – by hand! The disbelievers may be parents or teachers of five and six-year-olds (or even 11 and 12-year-olds, especially if the children are boys), or they may be the children themselves.

I usually ask teachers to give students a few sewing lessons before we make our quilt. More often than not, those "lessons" don't help. Adults usually assume that a child cannot handle a normal needle. Bigger is better, they think. When was the last time you tried sewing fabric with something the size of a knitting needle?

Young children are frequently given a huge craft or darning needle threaded with yarn and a piece of burlap or other loosely-woven material – sometimes construction paper with holes punched around the edge.

The method of choice seems to be the stab stitch – the needle goes in through the top, is then pulled all the way out the back, turned around and pushed in through the back, and pulled out through the front.

These first attempts may help eye-hand coordination, but you can't make a quilt that way.

Once you show a child how to make a running stitch on a straight line, that child will probably amaze you with tiny, accurate stitches. Boys seem especially proficient at sewing – more so than girls. Perhaps it has something to do with attention to detail, or fine motor control, but my theory is that boys know they're not supposed to sew – everyone has told them that. They're so nervous they do exactly what they're told – and consequently they make neat, accurate stitches. Girls, on the other hand, know that all girls sew (regrettably, very few do) and they pay little attention to directions. The result: hopelessly large stitches and terrible tangles!

There are, of course, notable exceptions. By the time kids reach high school, many girls can sew very well. Those girls who have never sewn by high school often have a hard time learning.

The trick to trouble-free sewing sessions is meticulous preparation, detailed instruction, plenty of volunteer help, and a liberal dash of humor.

PREPARATION

Making a successful quilt that fits together perfectly and hangs straight against the wall demands accurate cutting, marking and sewing.

Be sure that all your fabric squares are the correct size. With a sharp Number 2 pencil, carefully mark ¼-inch seam allowance lines on the back of all pieces to be joined. Adult quiltmakers use a Number 3 pencil to draw very lightly on their fabric. Children need to see the seam line quickly and easily, so make sure your line is fairly heavy. (For complete cutting and marking directions, see the Basic Quilting chapter.)

Use pins with colored plastic heads. Before the sewing session, carefully pin fabric squares together. The pin should be immediately below the line to be sewn. The pin should point from right to left, in the direction to be sewn. (You will need to reverse this direction for left-handed sewers.)

Needles should be threaded before the session. Pull a 36" length of thread from the spool, put it through the needle's eye, then make a small knot joining both loose ends together. The final doubled thread should be no more than 18" long, or it will become tangled and knotted very quickly.

EQUIPMENT

Needles: Use a good quality Number 7 Sharp sewing needle, a Number 9 Crewel needle, or a round-eyed sewing needle that is no more than 1½" long. Darning needles and other large-eyed craft needles (such as tapestry) are extremely hard to sew with. They may be easy to thread, but they are too thick to push through fabric layers. Needles that are extra-long make giant stitches. Generally, the smaller the needle, the smaller the stitches. Don't be surprised to find all the chrome has melted off the needles after a few sessions with sticky little fingers. Run the needles through an emery bag, or rub with extra find sandpaper to make them slip easily through fabric again. Children will bend needles very quickly, too, so have plenty of "spares."

One safety note about pins and needles: in a group, you'll often find one child (usually male) who delights in "grossing out" his friends by sewing his fingers. From the standpoint of basic hygiene, this should definitely be discouraged, especially if the same needles are being used by many different people. Threats of horrible diseases don't usually impress kids too much and may even backfire on you. (One district complained that my quilting project was "too dangerous" for children because of possible "needle pricks!") Instead, use humor, something like: "This isn't Brain Surgery 101," and the rest of the class will usually laugh at the kid, instead of being impressed by him. This should put a stop to the problem.

To keep the quilt clean, it's also a good idea to require children to wash their hands with soap before a sewing class, and after any major pin or needle pricks, just to be on the safe side.

Thread: Use a good quality white, natural colored or gray thread. The cheap five-for-a-dollar kind of thread tangles and knots very quickly during hand sewing.

Needle Threaders: These handy gadgets make needle-threading much faster for children and adults – but only if you know how to use them! Alas, they don't make 'em like they used to, and inexperienced hands can quickly destroy a whole package. Try wrapping the wire ends with several layers of duct tape or masking tape to anchor them into the handle.

Many packages do not come with directions. The thin wire loop is pushed through the needle's eye. Since it's fairly stiff, it should go through much more easily than the thread. The thread is then put through the large wire loop on the far side of the needle's eye. Holding hard to the wire where it's implanted in the "handle," draw the wire back through the needle's eye, pulling the thread along with it. (If you hold the threader just by its handle during this step, the wire is often pulled away from its anchor.) You may need to "jiggle" the wire a few times to coax the thread through. Remove the thread from the wire loop and your needle is quickly threaded!

Another quick way to thread needles is to cut your thread at an angle with very sharp scissors, keep it dry, hold it very close to the end to prevent splitting, and force it through the needle's eye.

Scissors: Use good quality sharp sewing scissors. Several companies now offer inexpensive, lightweight children's scissors, the kind with colored plastic handles and extra sharp blades. Keep your sewing scissors strictly for cutting thread and fabric. Cutting paper (or worse) will make them dull and useless for sewing.

Because these new style scissors are extremely sharp, you must keep an eye on your students and warn them of dire consequences if they play around with the blades. The only injury I've ever had in five years of teaching this project was a sliced finger – a third grader tried to wrestle the scissors from his neighbor by grabbing the blades and pulling.

Take time to do a "scissors safety" lecture: Always hold scissors by the handles. Always keep scissors closed when not in use. Never cut anything but thread or fabric with your scissors. Never grab scissors by their blades. Watch your knuckles when cutting. Keep scissors on the table at all times, unless they are being used to cut thread or fabric – NO idle opening and closing of scissors (a favorite child's pastime, I've found!).

You may choose to ban scissors use with very young children, or those who don't follow the rules. Let the volunteers have the scissors (wearing them on a ribbon around the neck keeps them handy), and make the children go to the adults to have thread cut.

Wouldn't it be simpler to find scissors that aren't so sharp? Possibly – but dull scissors don't cut thread, and your adult helpers will complain like crazy! The "safe" sewing scissors I bought for my first few school projects required several minutes of "hacking" to cut thread, left the thread too fuzzy to put into a needle, and were nearly all broken after a few months' use. I rest my case.

Pins: Pins with large colored heads are much easier to use than ordinary, all-metal heads. The colored heads are also useful to show children the direction they should sew.

Buy good quality, stainless steel pins. Cheap pins bend quickly, and some rust when exposed to the acid in the fabric dyed with powdered soft drink mix.

Pincushions: That old standby, the stuffed red "tomato" with its "strawberry" emery bag dangling off the side is an inexpensive catchall for pins and needles when children are sewing. If you insist that all pins and needles be "parked" in a pincushion when not in use, you'll have less trouble picking them out of carpeting, or off the floor!

You may choose to make your own pincushions, but they have a short life span when used with large groups of children. Most pincushions tend to "eat" needles; carefully press the cushion onto a hard surface and you may be surprised at how many buried needles reappear!

The dangling "strawberry" is filled with powdered emery, a type of crushed rock used to smooth and sharpen needles.

Baskets: Inexpensive, small plastic baskets make good "holdalls" for the sewing table. Shoeboxes, or disposable microwave baking containers could also be used. Divide your sewing group into tables of five or six, and place a basket at each table. Each basket should contain a pincushion (complete with six threaded needles), a needle threader, scissors and a spool of thread.

TEACHING CHILDREN TO SEW

When teaching children how to sew, start by giving a short lecture, explaining what they're going to do and why they have to do it in a particular way. Illustrate the talk with fabric examples.

Gear your talk to the age of the children. Use simple vocabulary for young children; be more technical with older ones. Add a little humor, so the talk doesn't get boring.

INTRODUCTION

Here's an introduction suitable for elementary school kids. "A quilt is like a puzzle – all the pieces have to fit together. The smaller pieces of fabric must first be stitched into a square or "block," and every block must be the same size, so it fits next to all the other blocks of the quilt.

"The first thing you'll notice about the piece you're given to sew is that there's a pin in it (hold up an example for children to see). This pin is very important. Do NOT take it out until you have sewn your pieces together. If it falls out before you're through, ask a helper to put it back for you. The pin is holding your two pieces of fabric in exactly the right way that they need to be sewn.

"You'll also notice that there are several lines drawn on your fabric. These are the lines we're going to sew on. How will we know which line to use? Look for the pin. The line that we sew is always the line above the pin – the line that's parallel to the pin, like railroad tracks.

"The pin is also like an arrow: the sharp end is the point, and the colored end is like the feathers. The arrow tells us which direction to sew – from the colored end towards the point (show an example).

"Now let's take a closer look at these lines. To make sure all the pieces fit perfectly, everyone must use the same seam allowance. The seam allowance is the distance from the edge of the fabric to the line on which you're going to sew. (Show an example). Our seam allowance is one-quarter of an inch.

"It's really important that everyone sews right on the line. Not above the line, not below the line – not around the line – but right ON the line! Every stitch must be right on the line.

"What will happen if some people stitch above the line? (Wait for an answer). The pieces may fall apart, because there's not enough fabric to hold the stitches in place.

"What will happen if some people stitch below the line? (Wait for answer). The finished pieces will be too small. Remember, we said every piece must be exactly the same size so all the pieces fit together. If we sew below the line, these pieces won't fit properly, and our block will have a hole in it.

"Remember, too, that we're only sewing one line at a time – we're not turning any corners. When we've stitched our seam, the pieces of fabric should open like a book. (Demonstrate). If we stitch around the corner, we'll have made a little pocket or a hat! The pieces won't open up.

"To make a quilt that will last a long time, do we need to sew with big stitches or little stitches? Look at your clothing; check the size of the stitches. (Wait for answers). We need SMALL stitches – teeny, tiny stitches, right on the line!

"When quilters make giant stitches, these are called "toe catchers." Why do you think they're called toe catchers? (Because, if you slept under this quilt, you could catch your toes in the giant stitches!)

"What happens when you make a toe catcher in your seam? The quilt blocks could fall apart, and you'll have a big gap in your seam. This is what I call "air conditioning!" If you can see a hole in the seam you've sewn, you've got air conditioning! All the stuffing will fall out of our quilt!

"When we start sewing, we have a needle on one end of our thread; what do we need on the other end? A knot! Why? Because, without a knot, the thread will pull out of the fabric and all the stitches will come undone.

"Now we're ready to sew with teeny-tiny stitches, right on the line. You may have learned to sew using a stab stitch: The needle goes in through the front, you pull it all the way through to the back, turn it around, poke it in the back, and pull it through to the front. It's very difficult to sew a straight line this way.

"We're going to use a running stitch, and once you get the hang of it, you'll find it's much faster. With a running stitch, just a little bit of the needle goes in through the front, scoops up a tiny bit of fabric, then pokes right back out to the front again – right on the line. In and out makes one stitch – not in and through to the back. (Demonstrate)

"To get tiny stitches, you only put the tip of the needle through the fabric – and bring it right back out again. If you put a whole lot of the needle through the fabric, you'll make a giant stitch. (Demonstrate)

"We sew all along the line with tiny running stitches – remember, we don't turn any corners – and then what do we do at the end? (Most kids will say you tie another knot). It's awfully difficult to tie a knot right against the fabric – what else could we do? What if we took some extra stitches, right on the line? Take three extra stitches, one right on top of the other, right on the line (an overcasting stitch).

"Now, carefully cut your thread, leaving a little tail. Don't cut the fabric by mistake. Park your needle in the pincushion. Now you can take out the pin, put it in the pincushion, and check your seam for air conditioning.

"The two pieces of fabric should open like a book (show example). Pull the two pieces slightly apart and look at your seam to make sure there are no gaps. If there are no holes, your piece is finished. Tie a knot on the end of your needle and thread, and you are ready to sew another piece.

"If there is air conditioning in your piece, tie a knot at the end of your thread and stitch over the gap. Take three stitches in place when you're finished, then cut your thread and check to make sure the air conditioning's gone."

DEMONSTRATION

Even the most attentive child won't know how to sew after a lecture. It's important to demonstrate the technique. I like to show each child, individually, by standing beside him or her and making the first few stitches. As each child is shown, the rest of the children in the group should watch carefully.

Start by showing the group which line to sew. Remind them to check the fabric frequently to be sure the back piece doesn't slip out of position while they're sewing. Tell them to check, too, that the needle is going through both pieces of fabric. The most beautiful stitching is no good if it doesn't hold the two layers together.

Hold the fabric in front of the first child with your left hand, then make the first stitch, starting from the top of the fabric, with your right hand. While you're making the stitch, say: "The needle goes in on the line, just a little bit goes through (show them the needle tip on the back side), and then it comes out again, right on the line. Then you pull to the end of the thread."

As you're making a second stitch, say: "The needle goes in on the line – a teeny tiny stitch – and the needle comes out on the line." Pull the thread through. Tuck the needle in to make a third stitch, and hand the work to the child to complete the stitch.

Stand over the child while the next couple of stitches are made, reminding everyone to keep the stitches really small, then move on to the next child and repeat the process.

For left-landed sewers (unless you're lucky enough to have a left-handed volunteer), reverse the direction of the pin (it will now point from left to right), hold the piece so the bulk of the material is at the top and the seam you are sewing is on the bottom, then stand in front of the child instead of beside him. You can then sew using your right hand, and the process will be visually correct for a "lefty."

One left-handed woman told me her right-handed mother taught her to sew sitting in front of a mirror. Somewhere there's an unwritten law that states the only left handed people are children. I rarely have left-handed adult volunteers – and never in the classes filled with left-handed children.

Individual demonstrations are really important. It's not enough to sit at one end of the table, showing kids what you want them to do. First, they can't see exactly what you're doing, and second, the way you're sewing is backwards for them! No wonder they make mistakes!

Take the time to work with each child, individually, and wait until you're sure that child knows how to make a stitch. Really small kids and those with handicaps may need you to hold their hands in yours and make the first stitches together. Children with impaired motor control or low vision can often sew successfully if you hold the fabric while they operate the needle. Sometimes, the stab stitch is easier for these children, while you hold the fabric tightly stretched.

When the first sewers get to the end of the seam line, you'll need to go back and demonstrate how to finish off. You may need to show the "finishing stitch" several times before the kids catch on. Keep encouraging them to make tiny stitches.

As they become more confident, children often speed up – and quality goes down. Tell children that how much they sew is not as important as how well they sew. Discourage "racing" – far better to have fewer pieces, beautifully stitched, than more pieces that have to be re-sewn!

Another word of caution: Some children are very happy to let somebody else finish off their piece, or fix their holes.

Encourage them to do their own work – they'll feel far more pride when they're finished.

VOLUNTEERS

Sewing with a group of children really requires plenty of adult supervision – especially if the children are young. Tiny tots may need one adult for every two or three children. Elementary children work best with no more than a five to one ratio.

Tangles and knots and skipped stitches are major mysteries to a novice sewer. Things that can be fixed in a jiffy by an experienced sewer are really discouraging for a child. Kids soon become frustrated if they have to wait in line for help.

Organize your sewing sessions by breaking the group into small clusters, with an adult working with each cluster. The adult fixes problems, demonstrates "finishing stitches," threads needles, ties knots and checks finished work for air conditioning.

Be sure each volunteer understands the system you're using. If you've described the running stitch and the volunteer is trying to teach the backstitch, the kids are going to be confused! Either train the adults before class, or have them listen to your lecture and stand behind you while you demonstrate. They can then go to their own small groups and carry on.

THE "BOSS" SYSTEM

When making a group quilt, somebody has to be "The Boss." One person has to know where everything goes and how everything fits together.

When I work with a group, I have a highly organized system that works efficiently for everyone.

First, I break the class into small groups, depending on the number of volunteers available (ideally, one adult to no more than five children). Each group sits at a separate table, complete with one adult and a basket of sewing equipment.

I sit at the head of the room at my own table. On the table I have an ironing area, pins, scissors, pieces of the quilt, and three small, different colored plastic baskets.

The "Out" basket contains the pieces that are ready to sew, all carefully pinned together. The "In" basket is empty – this will be used for finished work. The third basket is the "Help!" basket – that's where I toss pieces that need to be re-sewn or taken apart and done again.

Once I have completed my lecture and demonstrations for each child, I sit alone at my worktable. When a piece is finished, the child drops it in the "In" basket and takes a new piece from the "Out" basket.

I check each seam for accuracy, iron seam allowances when necessary or trim blocks to size, find the next piece of fabric that matches, and pin the new pieces together. The newly-pinned work then goes back in the "Out" basket, ready to be sewn.

When I find particularly good sewers, I give them pieces to fix from the "Help!" basket.

It's a good, rotating system as long as I don't get behind in my work. As children gain confidence, they sew a lot faster, and I'm often pinning at top speed to keep the "Out" basket filled for them!

If your group quilt involves more than one class, be sure to allow enough time between sessions to get all the needles threaded, and all the work ironed, trimmed and pinned for the next bunch of kids!

Using this very organized system, 100 children divided into four, 45-minute classes can sew all the 9-patch blocks and join them into rows for a large Flavor Quilt – by hand – in two days.

Keep calm, keep organized – and keep your sense of humor!

Be sure to read through the Basic Quilting chapter and The Large Quilt chapter for specific instructions on cutting, marking, pinning and sewing.

A Quick Basic Quilting Course

The same people who say, "I've always wanted to make a quilt," are often the ones who say, "I had no idea it could be so easy!" at the end of a week-long project.

If making quilts conjures up visions of painstakingly cutting and hand sewing thousands of tiny scraps of fabric, think again. Most women threw away their wood cooking stoves and their washboards several generations ago, and feeling you have to make quilts "the old way" means you're living in a time warp!

Today's quiltmakers have a dizzying array of timesaving gadgets at their fingertips, and new techniques for cutting and sewing. Almost every quilt pattern ever invented can now be sewn in a fraction of the time it once took, and with far greater accuracy.

First, get rid of the notion that "real quilts" are stitched entirely by hand. Do you think pioneer women would have sewn by hand if somebody had given them a sewing machine? With all the other back-breaking work they had to do, they would surely have put a timesaving invention to good use!

There's still a place in our lives for heirloom-quality hand sewing, but most mothers and teachers don't have the time to create such masterpieces.

In this chapter, basic quiltmaking techniques will be covered to prepare the reader for making a large Flavor Quilt. The actual quilt top construction and completion of the quilt are covered in the chapter entitled "The Large Flavor Quilt."

Read this chapter before you start making the quilt, then refer to the Large Quilt chapter for step-by-step directions.

TOOLS

New timesaving tools for quiltmaking are constantly appearing on the market. Unless you live in a major metropolitan area with access to a good fabric or quilt shop, the best way to keep current is to get on the mailing list of one of the many mail-order catalogs (see "Sources & Resources" chapter). Some of the best tools are not sold in every fabric shop or discount store.

The rotary cutter has revolutionized quiltmaking. With this tool, it's possible to cut out an entire quilt in less time than it used to take to cut a few blocks.

A *rotary cutter* looks like a small pizza cutter, but the circular blade is razor-sharp. There are several designs available, but the easiest to use consists of a straight plastic handle with either a small or large cutting wheel protected by a plastic sheath.

One brand has a safety shield that must be manually pulled and pushed to expose and cover the blade. Another brand has a spring-loaded safety shield that automatically retracts when the blade is pressed into the fabric. This safety shield is vitally important, since the rotary cutter blade is dangerously sharp. Never leave a blade open, even for a moment! Get into the habit of opening the blade when it's actually in the fabric, and closing it immediately after each cut is made. With the spring-loaded model, the blade is always covered by the safety shield, except when actually in use.

Do not leave the rotary cutter where children or curious adults can play with it! This is a wonderful tool, but it must be used with the proper care to avoid accidents.

Because a rotary cutter is so sharp, many layers of fabric can be cut easily with one stroke. A special rubber mat is required for use under the fabric. Don't try to use anything else for a cutting surface, or you will damage both the blade and the cutting surface.

The cutting mats come in many sizes and several types, some with a preprinted grid to make accurate cutting easier. All of these mats are heat-sensitive. Never leave a cutting mat in a hot car or on any heated surface, or it will be permanently damaged. A warped cutting mat makes it impossible to cut accurate quilt pieces. Once a mat is warped, it's virtually impossible to flatten it.

As with all tools, buy the best that you can afford. There are less expensive models of both cutters and mats on the market, but they may not be as satisfactory as a more expensive type.

Keep the blade sharp, and replace it when it becomes dull or starts skipping. If you accidentally cut over a pin, or other hard object, you may damage the blade. Synthetic fabrics also will dull the blade faster than natural fabrics.

Unfortunately, most rotary cutters do not come with instructions. If you have never used one before, ask for a demonstration at the store when you buy it, or take a class from an experienced quilter.

Templates and *rulers* must be used with a rotary cutter to cut accurate pieces of cloth. A template is a pattern shape. You cut around the edge of a template to make pieces for a quilt, much the same as a cookie cutter is used to cut cookies.

There are many metal and heavy plastic templates available from quilt stores and mail-order houses for various quilt patterns. The most useful multipurpose cutting edge is one of the many varieties of heavy plastic rulers. The best quilting rulers come in various widths and lengths, but should have multiple markings on the surface, preferably every 1/8" in both directions. Various angles are also useful on the surface of the ruler.

If you plan to buy only one quilting ruler, make sure it is at least 24" long and about 6" wide. You can also buy large and small squares, which are extremely useful for trimming finished quilt blocks.

Some rulers come with a non-slip surface on one side. Others tend to "skate" over the surface of the cloth, and must be anchored by heavy hand pressure. You can also purchase stick-on strips of sandpaper which will help prevent slipping.

When the rotary cutter first came on the market, many women borrowed their husbands' metal right-angle carpentry rulers to use as cutting edges. Though awkward and heavy, one of these is still a possibility, if you cannot find a quilt ruler. The cutting edge should be perfectly straight and accurate. Don't use a wooden ruler or a thin plastic ruler because the rotary blade will easily cut through them.

USING A ROTARY CUTTER

Cutting with a rotary cutter is faster than using scissors, once you get the hang of it. If you are right-handed, hold the ruler in place by pressing down on it with your left hand. Holding the whole hand flat on the ruler gives better control than just using the fingertips. Be sure your knuckles are safely away from the cutting edge.

If you have trouble with your ruler slipping out of position, try dropping the tip of your little finger off the left-hand edge, onto the fabric or mat. This helps to "anchor" the ruler. If you're cutting a very long line, it sometimes helps to move your left hand down the ruler as you cut. Be sure the ruler stays in the correct position while you do this.

Hold the rotary cutter in your right hand, with the blade perpendicular to the edge of the ruler. Most cutters have a ridged area on the handle, just above the blade, for your index finger. If you have the type of cutter that has a manually-operated safety cover, use your thumb to operate the safety latch. If you find it too hard to operate the safety, try adjusting the screw that holds the blade assembly in place. If you loosen the nut just slightly, the safety latch will be easier to operate.

Cut fabric by rolling the cutter blade against the edge of the ruler. The blade should be straight up and down, perpendicular to your fabric. Pull the blade slightly towards the ruler's edge as you cut. Many people roll the blade away from the body, but some people find it easier to control the blade by pulling towards the body.

Use gentle pressure with your index finger and wrist, depending on the number of layers you are cutting. The heaviest pressure should feel no harder than cutting through a block of cheddar cheese. If you have a new blade and only one or two layers of fabric, a gentle pressure should easily cut. If you put too much pressure on the cutter, or if you try to cut too fast, you're likely to pull away from the ruler and cut a crooked line. With practice, you will soon know how much pressure it takes.

After you have cut your line, keep your left hand in position on the ruler, then with your right hand, immediately put the safety latch on to cover your blade. Set your cutter aside and gently move the bulk of the fabric away from the newly cut edge to make sure you have cut through all layers. If you have missed a spot, go back and cut through it. If you have cut through the layers, remove the ruler and check your strip

for accuracy.

Be sure you have a clear cutting space, with nothing caught under your fabric. Avoid awkward cutting situations, like trying to cut sideways, or crossing your hands! This is one way that accidents happen. If you are right-handed, the bulk of the fabric will be on your left when you trim edges, and on your right when you cut strips. You can either move around the table until you are in the correct cutting position, or, holding your fabric in place on the cutting mat, gently swivel the mat around, moving the fabric with it.

If you plan to continue cutting strips from a piece of folded fabric at a later date, put two or three pins in the fabric to hold the cut edge exactly in place. Then you won't have to straighten your fabric every time you begin cutting.

SEWING MACHINES

You can take much of the drudgery out of quiltmaking by using a sewing machine, though there are still many who prefer to hand piece. Children can easily sew small blocks for a quilt by hand, but when it comes to adding long lattice strips and borders, a sewing machine is far more accurate. It's really hard to sew a long, straight line by hand.

Any machine in good working order can be used to make a quilt. If you have the time to teach them, children can also learn to sew by machine. They'll require constant supervision. Adjust the sewing speed to "slow" while the child is learning to "steer" the fabric under the needle.

If your machine does not have an adjustable speed on the sewing head, check the foot pedal. Some machines have a "plus" or "minus" screw under the foot, which controls the sewing speed. If your foot pedal is the metal kind that looks like an oversized clothespin, try putting a foam hair curler inside the "clip" portion. When the child "floors" the machine, the foam roller will keep the speed fairly slow.

Most quiltmakers use the edge of their presser foot as a guide for sewing straight seams. The universal seam allowance for quiltmaking is ¼". Many sewing machines have an all-purpose foot that makes a perfect ¼" seam. However, some machines have a foot that is either wider, or narrower than ¼". You can check your foot by measuring from the needle to the right-hand edge of the foot, or, more accurately, by sewing on a piece of paper with no thread in the needle. Guide the edge of the paper along the edge of the foot, then measure from the needle holes to the edge.

Some machines have several needle positions. If your machine foot is not a perfect ¼", try adjusting the needle position. Look for a different foot in your accessories. If all else fails, stick a piece of tape onto your machine plate at the ¼" seam mark and use it as a sewing guide.

If you are finishing a children's quilt that has been partially sewn by hand, be sure to follow the marked seam lines on the blocks, so that all the blocks will be the same size.

When it comes to machine quilting, a special "walking foot" or "even-feed foot" may be required to reduce puckering of the layers. Check with your local sewing machine dealer to get such a foot for your machine, or try the mail-order catalogues. Some machines have a special quilting foot.

You may need to reduce the pressure on the foot for quilting. Look in your machine's instruction book under "darning" or "embroidery" to find out how to do this. Some machines have a numbered wheel inside the head to reduce pressure; others have a pop-up screw on top of the head, rather like the timer devices in turkeys; some have a built-in system that

makes allowances for the thicker layers; and still others have a screw inside the head that needs to be adjusted to reduce the pressure. Just be sure to put the pressure back to "normal" when you're finished quilting or your regular sewing will slide all over the place!

To learn more about machine piecing and machine quilting, see the "Sources & Resources" chapter for suggested reading, or contact your local quilt shop, quilt guild or library.

THREAD

Choosing the right thread is important when making a quilt. For piecing the quilt top, either by hand or machine, buy a good quality sewing thread in a neutral color. Gray is a good, all-purpose color that doesn't show through a Flavor Quilt. Avoid the very cheap polyester thread (it tangles and shreds too easily) and don't use very old thread – it breaks.

The quilting thread that is on the market is meant for hand quilting only. It's too heavy for piecing, and it causes major tension problems in a sewing machine. Stick to regular "all-purpose" thread for quilt construction. If you plan to quilt by hand, be sure to use quilting thread. Regular sewing thread is not usually strong enough to use for quilting, unless you wax it.

Many machine quilters use invisible nylon thread. This is not the "nightmare" nylon we all grew to hate 10 or 20 years ago. This new version is as thin as hair, soft and very pliable, not thick and wiry. Use it only on top of the machine, never in the bobbin! Regular sewing thread in the bobbin works best for machine quilting. Don't use the nylon thread for piecing – just for quilting.

The nylon thread comes in clear or smoke (brown). Use the smoke color on everything except pure white or very pale pastels. The clear nylon picks up and reflects light. Used on darker fabrics it tends to "twinkle." The smoke thread is truly invisible, giving only the appearance of quilting, without any stitches showing.

The advantage of using invisible thread is that you don't have to keep changing quilting thread to match the quilt top. If you prefer, a neutral sewing thread can be used for machine quilting. The machine quilting referred to in this book is "in the ditch" – stitched right in the seam, so it is virtually invisible on the quilt top.

FABRIC

In the tradition of thrifty pioneers who "made do" with what they had when making quilts, many of today's quiltmakers feel pressure to use up all the fabric they own before buying more.

In many cases, "making do," or "buying cheap" is false economy. The time spent in making a quilt is the same, whether you use good fabric or poor fabric. The results, however, are another matter. Not only is low-grade fabric harder to work with, but it also doesn't look as nice in a finished quilt.

Don't be fooled by appearances. The bargain-priced fabric you find in a discount store or on a closeout table, may look exactly like fabric you have seen at twice the price in a quilt shop. The pattern is the same, the color identical – but it's half the price. Is it the same fabric? Probably not. Fabric manufacturers often run several grades for sale to different markets. The best quality fabric costs more. The thinner, poorer quality fabric is cheaper.

Check the fabric specifications for the projects in this book, and buy the best you can afford.

All fabric for quiltmaking should be washed before use. Washing in hot water removes excess dye and chemicals, and shrinks the fabric to its true size. If you plan to use the fabric with dyes, paints, crayons and dye sticks, remember not to add bleach or fabric softener to the wash water, as these will repel the colors. If you use a detergent, check to be sure it does not contain bleach or fabric softener.

Iron the fabric before cutting. Many fabrics are easier to press if ironed while still damp. Keep large amounts of fabric on a cardboard bolt board to prevent wrinkling.

Prepare fabric for strip cutting by snipping about an inch from the edge, and ripping across the width, from selvage to selvage, to get the straight cross grain of the goods. You can prevent waste by asking to have your fabric ripped, instead of cut, when you buy it. Most quilt stores rip fabric; most fabric stores do not. Since the fabrics used in quilts are usually 100% cotton, or a cotton/polyester blend, there should be minimal damage from ripping. This "fuzzy" edge will be trimmed off, anyway.

CUTTING FABRIC

Using a rotary cutter and mat with a quilting ruler, quilt pieces can be quickly and easily cut. First, cut the fabric into strips, then stack the strips together and re-cut into squares, rectangles, triangles, or whatever shape your pattern requires. If you are cutting squares for hand-sewing a Flavor Quilt, mark a seam line on each strip before you cut to save marking time later.

BASIC STRIPS
• Rip fabric from selvage to selvage to find the cross grain. Fold the fabric in half, so the two selvages are together (the way it's folded on the bolt), and match the ripped edge. Iron the folded fabric, pressing a crease at the fold. Don't worry if the selvages don't match down the length of the fabric. The grain on today's fabric is rarely true in both directions. Press the crease

FLAVOR QUILTS

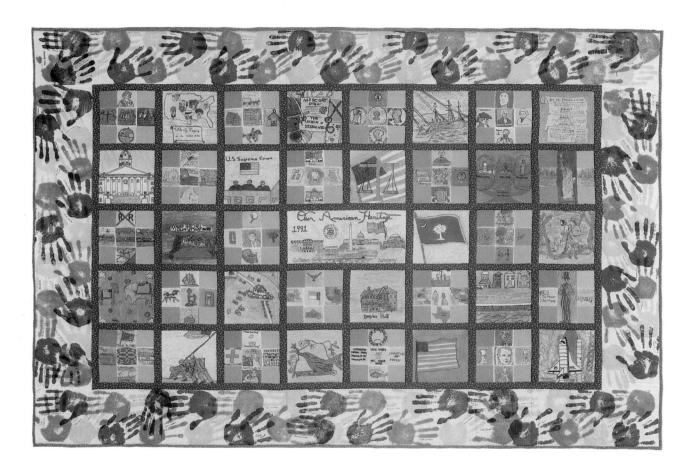

OUR AMERICAN HERITAGE QUILT by Calhoun Academy, St. Matthews, SC, March, 1991.
Seventh, ninth and eleventh grade students created the quilt as a history and government project. Two ninth grade students created the center block, which depicts familiar Washington landmarks. Fine details were added to the fabric crayons with a permanent pen.

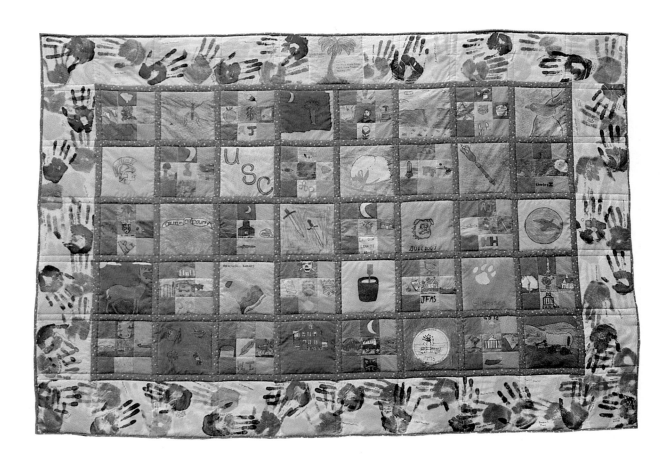

THE SOUTH CAROLINA HISTORY QUILT
by John Ford Middle School, St. Matthews, SC,
January, 1990.
This eighth grade library project followed a unit
on state history.

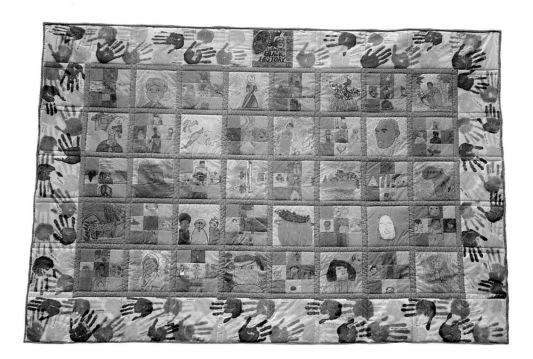

THE BLACK HISTORY QUILT
by Lewis Greenview Elementary School,
Columbia, SC, February, 1991.
Third grade students studied people and events
in Afro-American history, then used bright colors
and patterns to illustrate their quilt.

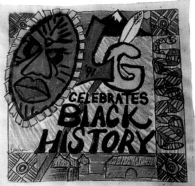

The original drawing for the Black History
Quilt dedication block is on the left, with
the design transferred to fabric on the right.
A permanent pen is used to highlight the
details. Note the reverse image process
required for printing letters and numbers.

CELEBRATING THE 1890'S
by Rama Road Elementary School, Charlotte,
NC, January, 1990.
Second grade students learned about their com-
munity's unique history before making this quilt
to mark the hundredth anniversary of their
school. The project was organized by parent vol-
unteers Ann Hollowell and Benita Bryson, both
quilters, and completed in two all-day work-
shops.

THE SPACE QUILT (detail)
by Joseph Keels Elementary School,
Columbia, SC, October, 1990.
Fifth grade students produced a space quilt
to culminate a school-wide science unit.
The highlight of the space study unit and the
quilt project was a visit by NASA astronaut
Charles Bolden, who autographed his
own special block.

**THE ORANGEBURG QUILT by summer workshop
participants at the Orangeburg Arts Council,
Orangeburg, SC, June 1990.**
*This quilt was created by children from
preschool through high school as part of a
summer workshop program for the public.
The quilt depicts area events, landmarks,
industries, history and recreation.*

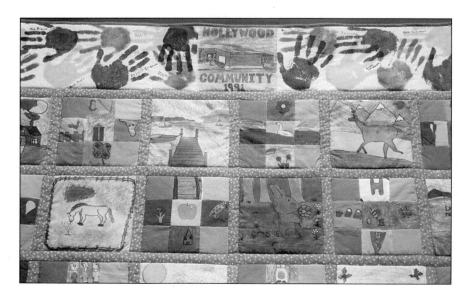

**HOLLYWOOD COMMUNITY QUILT
by Hollywood Elementary
School, Saluda, SC, January,
1991.**
*Fourth, fifth and seventh
graders drew pictures of their
rural community for a quilt.
Many of the teachers and parent
volunteers were also graduates
of this tiny country school.*

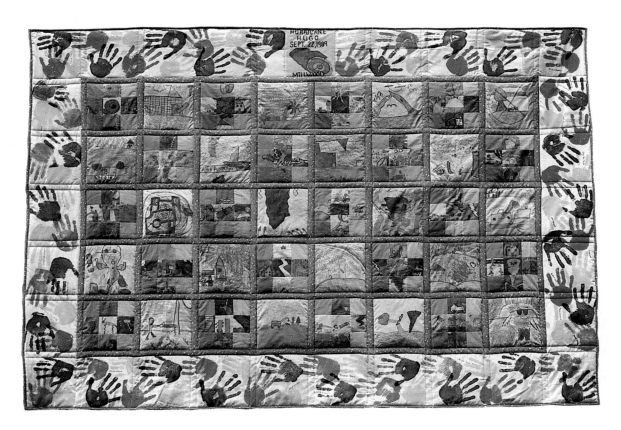

**HURRICANE HUGO QUILT by Millwood
Elementary School, Sumter, SC, April
1990.**

*Though far inland, Sumter was right in
the path of Hurricane Hugo (1989) as it
cut through the Carolinas. Third graders
at Millwood Elementary School drew
their impressions of the storm in a
commemorative quilt. Lightning, funnel
clouds, splintered trees and power lines,
wrecked cars and houses were all things
the third graders remembered.
They also drew caricatures of "Hugo"
as a hairy "dude" in sunglasses.*

**THE FOSSIL QUILT (detail) by Dent Middle School,
Columbia, SC, April, 1990.**

*Earth science teacher Dr. Arlene Marturano thought
a quilt would be the ideal way to show off her
students' new-found knowledge of fossils.
Students created their quilt drawings as a homework assigment. Only the pictures that rated an "A"
made it into the quilt. In a one-day workshop,
eighth grade students created a spectacular record
of prehistoric times. The quilt was on public view
for three months at the South Carolina State
Museum as part of the special exhibit,
"South Carolina: Through the Needle's Eye."*

CHARLOTTE'S WEB QUILT (detail) by Nursery Road Elementary School, Irmo, SC, October, 1989.
Third grade students read the children's classic, then illustrated a quilt with pigs and spiders – just in time for the South Carolina State Fair. The art teacher did a wonderful job of blending fabric crayon colors for the dedication block.

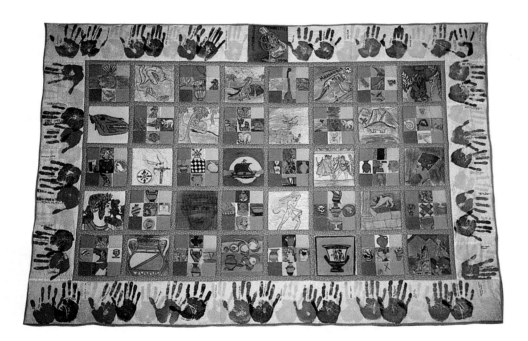

THE SCIENCE/HUMANITIES QUILT by Wil Lou Gray Opportunity School, Columbia, SC, December, 1990.
Thirty students at the state-run residential facility for troubled teens combined two themes into a single quilt. Most of the girls lost interest in the project, but several of the older boys became so involved that they requested permission to miss regular classes to finish the designs and sew the quilt together.

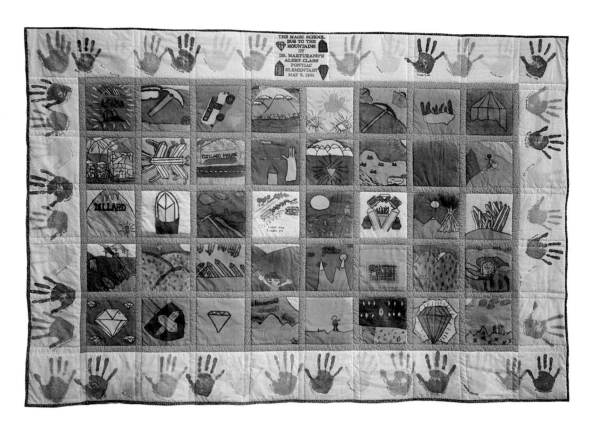

THE ROCK AND MINERAL QUILT by Pontiac Elementary School, Pontiac, SC, May, 1991.
Forty fourth and fifth grade students in the ALERT gifted and talented program created designs for this quilt on the bus trip home from a two-day rock hunting trip in the mountains. ALERT teacher Dr. Arlene Marturano created an irresistible study program, including designing and sewing nugget bags, "Jell-O® Geology" (edible "sedimentary rock"), games, "rock" music, field trips and finally a rock-hunting expedition followed by two days of quiltmaking and a public exhibit of the quilt and rock collections.

T-SHIRTS by participants in a one-day workshop sponsored by the Summer Arts Series for Youth (SASY), Tryon, NC, June, 1990.
Noah Carbone of Lancaster, SC; Jonathan Monk of Columbia, SC; and Nova McCune of Greer, SC decorated T-shirts with fabric paint, crayons and dye sticks at a one-day workshop.

COLONIAL LIFE QUILT, by Newell Elementary School, Charlotte, NC, December, 1988.
Third and fourth grade students studied Colonial life and regional history for an entire semester before making this quilt, which won a blue ribbon at the Charlotte Quilters' Guild show.

SENIOR ART PROJECT at Hilton Head High School, Hilton Head, SC, May 1989.
Bold colors were chosen for art students at Hilton Head High School to make a series of quilted banners. Design elements were limited to squares or triangles.

Many of the boys chose strong contrasts for their designs. The lightning bolt block was created by members of the school wrestling team, none of whom had ever sewn before.

A wide range of colors and designs, some traditional, some contemporary, reflect the students' interests.

CAROLYN BOGLE'S QUILT by the 1988 pre-first class at Kilbourne Park School, Columbia, SC, May, 1988.
This thank-you gift for a special teacher has a fabric crayon drawing and heart made by each child, a set of hand-prints, and commercial fabric for the lattice strips. Machine quilting outlines the designs.

WORK IN PROGRESS at Savannah Grove Elementary School, Florence, SC.
Muslin squares dyed in powdered soft drink mix drying. The flavors shown are cherry, orange, lemon-lime and grape.

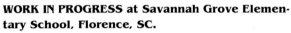

**BLOCKS from
South Kilbourne Elementary
School, Columbia, SC,
February, 1991.**
Fourth grade students made larger versions of the miniature Flavor Quilt. They used fabric crayons and paints, with quilting stitches to separate the designs.

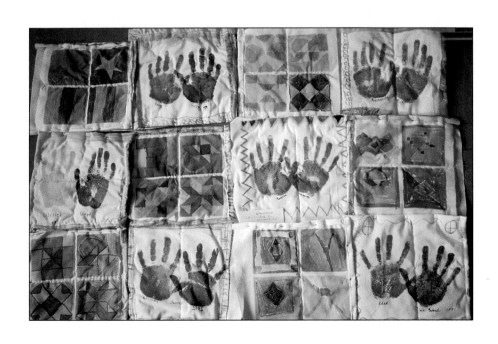

THE WHAT MAKES ME HAPPY QUILT by Richardson Primary School, Port Gibson, MS, 1991.
Sponsored by Mississippi: Cultural Crossroads. Resource person Megan Sweeney showed the third grade students how to use fabric crayons, dyes, batik and fabric paint to create this first in a series of quilts.
Photo: Patricia Crosby

THE SELF-PORTRAIT QUILT, entitled Here I Am!, by Richardson Primary School, Port Gibson, MS.
This is the second Mississippi: Cultural Crossroads quilt made by third graders at Richardson Primary under the guidance of Megan Sweeney. She says the project was inspired by the 1990 American Quilter magazine article about drink-mix dyed fabric quilts.
Photo: Patricia Crosby

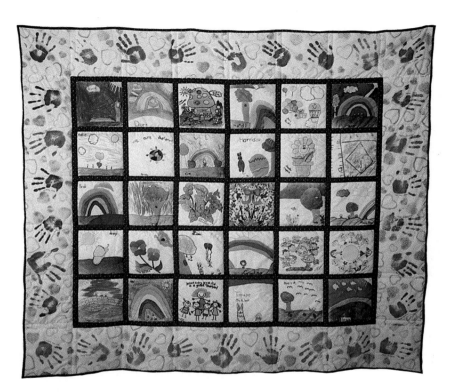

**SPRING FANTASY by Debby Griffis and the second-grade class at
Nursery Road Elementary School, Columbia, SC, Spring 1991.**
*Second graders, teachers and parent volunteers used fabric crayons to
draw pictures for this memory quilt presented to second-grade teacher
Mrs. Carol Sommers. Sponge shapes and cookie cutters were used to
decorate the handprint border. Debby Griffis, whose daughter Lisa was
a student in the class, pieced and quilted the wallhanging by machine.*

LISA'S QUILT (front view, right, and back view, above), 48" x 48", Ruth V. Irwin of Austin, TX, 1990.
Ruth experimented with fabric crayons after taking the author's workshop at the 1989 AQS show in Paducah, KY. Photo: Ruth Irwin

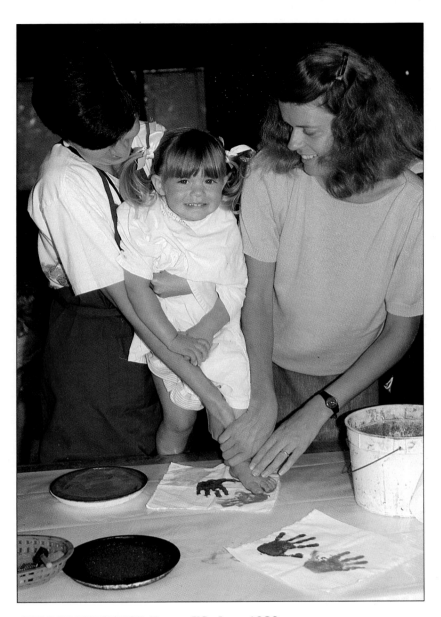

ONE-DAY WORKSHOP, Tryon, NC, June 1989.
*Handprints and footprints decorated miniature quilts made by
pre-schoolers and their parents at a one-day summer workshop in
Tryon, NC, in June, 1989. Some of the little ones didn't like the
feel of paint on their feet.*

THE KERSHAW ELEMENTARY QUILT, made by the entire school, Kershaw, SC, November, 1987.
Two extra rows were added to the basic quilt design to accommodate all the students in grades three, four, and five.

down the entire length of the fabric to be cut (Diagram 10-1).

- Carefully fold the fabric in half again, keeping the ripped cross-grain perfectly even and matching the first folded edge to the two selvages. Don't worry if the folded edge and the selvages don't match; it's the ripped cross-grain edge we're worrying about. Press a fold again. You should now have a long, narrow piece of folded fabric, about 11" wide, with four layers (Diagram 10-2).

- If you are right-handed, position the folded fabric on your cutting mat with the bulk of the fabric at your left. (If you have a large amount of fabric, gently "accordion" pleat it into a manageable bundle at the end of the table.) Use the right angle corner of your quilting ruler to line up exactly with the folded edges of the fabric, close to the ripped edge. Don't use the selvages as your guide, because they won't be straight. Holding the rotary cutter perpendicular to the ruler's edge, trim off the "fuzzy" edge and discard (Diagram 10-3).

- Without disturbing this newly-cut edge (pin the layers, if necessary), swivel your mat and fabric around so the bulk of the fabric is now on your right. You can also walk around to the other side of the table to achieve this maneuver.

- Using the cut edge of the fabric as your guide, measure the appropriate strip width with your ruler. Make sure the short edge of the ruler is lined up with the folded edges of the fabric to get a true, right-angle cut. Cut a strip of fabric. (Diagram 10-4)

- Open up your strip to make sure it's straight. If there's a "V" in the middle, your fabric was not cut at a right angle to the fold. Open up the fabric, rip, fold, iron and try again.

- Using the cut edge of your fabric as a

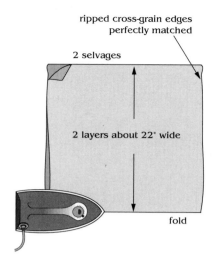

DIAGRAM 10-1
Fold fabric in half, matching ripped cross grain edge. Press a crease on the fold.

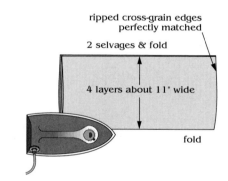

DIAGRAM 10-2
Fold fabric in half again, to make four layers. Press crease on the fold.

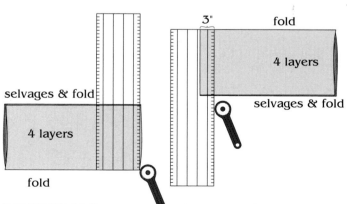

DIAGRAM 10-3
Line up right-angle bottom of ruler with fold. Use rotary cutter to trim off "fuzzy" edge.

DIAGRAM 10-4
Turn fabric so folds are at the top. Line up ruler with cut edge and folded edge to make a right angle. Cut strip.

guide, you can continue to cut strips along the length of the folded fabric. Every few cuts, it's a good idea to line up the right-angle edge of your ruler with the folded edge, and the left-hand edge of the ruler with the cut edge of the fabric, to make sure you're cutting straight strips. If necessary, trim off a wedge-shaped sliver to straighten your cut fabric.

CUTTING AND MARKING QUILT SQUARES

Multiple squares can be quickly cut from strips. If you mark a seam allowance on the strips, you can save much time later.

- Rip the fabric from selvage to selvage on the cross grain, as before. Matching the ripped edge, fold the fabric in half, matching selvages, the way the fabric is folded on the bolt. Iron the folded edge along the length of the fabric.

- Place the fabric on the cutting board, as before, and trim off the ripped edge. Remember, you will have only two layers of fabric this time, and the fabric will measure about 22" wide. Swing the fabric around, as before, so the bulk of it is on the right.

- Use a sharp #2 pencil to draw a line on the fabric ¼" from the cut edge. To keep the pencil line thin, roll the pencil between your fingertips as you draw, twisting the point from one side to the other, and it will stay sharp. Quiltmakers generally use a hard #3 pencil for marking fabric, but children need the darker line of the softer pencil.

- Using the cut edge of the fabric as a guide, measure the width of the strip and cut.

- Carefully turn the strip over and mark the ¼" seam line along the same edge as before. (When the strip is opened, the seam line should be continuous along one side.)

- Mark and cut as many strips as necessary

for the project. Carefully stack the strips together, matching both ends and edges. Make three stacks with no more than five folded strips in each stack. Line the stacks up so they are all perfectly even.

- Use the horizontal lines on your ruler to make sure the strip stacks are straight. Make a perpendicular cut close to the strip ends to remove all the selvages (Diagram 10-5). Carefully swing the cutting board around, or move to the other side of the table.

- Use the horizontal lines on the ruler and the newly cut ends of the strips to cut the appropriate size squares. Continue cutting until all the strips have been cut. Open up the "leftovers" at the fold and check to see if they are big enough to make a square. If you have layered five folded strips, you will have 10 squares in each small stack. Keep track of the number you have cut by turning each stack of 10, alternating first a square-shaped stack, then diamond-shaped, in a pile.

- Large squares can be cut the same way as small ones, with careful attention to matching edges when you stack the strips. If your quilt ruler is not wide enough to cut a big square, use a second ruler, either side-by-side with the first, or turned horizontally to the first, to form a right angle. (Diagram 10-6)

FABRIC GRAIN

You don't need an advanced degree in textiles to make a quilt, but it is helpful to understand the limitations of your fabric.

Give yourself a crash course in grain by pulling on a piece of fabric. When you pull the fabric from selvage to selvage on the cross grain, notice there is some "give" or stretch. Pull fabric on the lengthwise grain, as it comes off the bolt, and you'll notice there's hardly any give or stretch. Pull the fabric on the bias or diagonal, and you'll

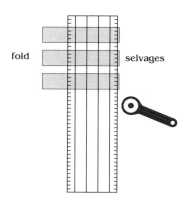

DIAGRAM 10-5
Use horizontal lines on ruler to cut straight edge of strips.

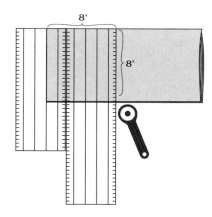

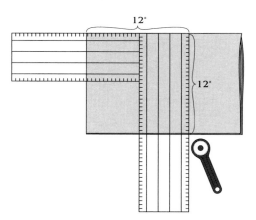

DIAGRAM 10-6
To cut strips or shapes wider than your ruler, use two rulers side-by-side, or turned at right angles to each other.

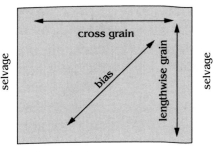

DIAGRAM 10-7
Test the grain by pulling the fabric in different directions.

find the most stretch of all. (Diagram 10-7)

Some professional quiltmakers insist that the only proper way to cut strips is on the lengthwise grain, where there is no "give" or stretch. This is fine if you are an extremely accurate seamstress. Unfortunately, if you're less than accurate, lengthwise strips don't give you any "fudge" room. It's hard to "ease" a lengthwise grain piece of fabric if it's too short, or a little too long.

Fabric cut on the crosswise grain, however, is much more forgiving. If one piece doesn't quite fit next to its neighbor, fabric cut on the cross grain can be gently persuaded to stretch or bunch up just enough to make a perfect match.

Fabric cut on the bias (the diagonal) is the stretchiest of all. It's bias-cut fabric that's used for most types of bindings and for things like collars, because the stretchy nature of the cloth allows it to curve around corners and into tight places.

Cutting strips of fabric on the cross grain, and then recutting the strips into squares, means that most of the pieces of the quilt will fit together without any problems. However, if you cut some strips on the cross grain, and others on the lengthwise grain, you may run into trouble getting pieces to fit exactly. It's a good idea to stick with either one direction or the other.

Special care must be exercised when working with bias edges, such as the long, diagonal sides of triangles. If children are sewing triangles, be sure that they don't stretch the bias seams, either in the sewing or in the ironing. A stretched bias will distort the quilt block. Often a stretched bias seam will "pooch" out, and refuse to stay flat, no matter how many times it's steam pressed. Fabric that has been badly stretched on the bias edge should be washed to see if it will regain its shape. If it's still distorted, discard the pieces and cut new ones.

MARKING FABRIC

TOOLS

Many marking tools are available to quiltmakers, ranging from colored chalk to pencils to chemical pens with ink that magically disappears within a few hours.

It's always a good idea to make a test of your marking tool on a scrap of fabric to see that it will do what it claims. A marking instrument should either be permanent and non-bleeding, or easily removable with water.

Perhaps the simplest marking tool is an ordinary pencil. Quiltmakers normally use a very sharp, hard #3 pencil to get an extremely fine line on fabric. This type of pencil can be used to mark seam lines for hand sewing, but should never to be used to mark a quilting design. The pencil lines will stay in the cloth, and may still be visible when the quilting is complete. A masterpiece quilt with pencil lines showing will never win a ribbon in a major show!

To make heavier and easier-to-see lines for children, I use a sharp #2 pencil to mark seam allowances. Never use a pen or similar marking tool that may bleed when it gets wet.

The cheapest marking tool for dark fabric is a very thin sliver of soap. You can sharpen the edge of your soap sliver by running it through the notch of a plastic bread bag tag.

The disadvantage of soap is that the mark rubs off quite easily. For a more stable line, try using a white, yellow, blue or silver pencil, available at quilt stores and art stores. Keep the pencil sharpened to give a fine line. Avoid the dressmaker type chalk pencils sold in many fabric stores. They break constantly and are impossible to keep sharp. The line they make is much too thick.

The various types of powdered chalk marking tools available give excellent and accurate lines, but are not really suitable for children's sewing since they rub off easily.

There are several types of felt-tipped marking pens for quilters. The best-known is the "blue" pen, which gives a bright blue line. To remove the line, you dip the fabric in cold water. Be sure to do a "test run" on the fabric you plan to use, because the blue pen sometimes does not come out in cold water. Never iron blue pen marks, or they may be permanently set in the fabric. Some detergents can also react with the chemicals and make the pen marks permanent.

Since the blue pen requires washing to remove it, it is not suitable for use with the Flavor Quilt. Wetting the quilt to remove the pen lines will also wet the fabric dyed in soft drink mix, and the squares will lose some of their intensity.

Another type of chemical pen has purple ink which fades away after a short period of time. This is the kind that I use to mark the Flavor Quilt for quilting.

The disadvantage of the purple pen is that it sometimes disappears before you want it to, especially in humid weather. Some quilters have also discovered that both the blue and the purple pen can reappear in their quilts in very humid weather. That's why it's always wise to try a "test" on a scrap of fabric before you use any marking tool on your quilt.

A newer chemical pen is pink, and has a built-in "remover." When you're ready to remove the pink lines, you draw over them with the "remover" tip and they disappear. Sometimes the remover leaves a yellowish residue on the fabric, so again, try a test before you use it.

MARKING QUILT SQUARES

Before marking seam allowances on your quilt squares for the projects in this book, look at a diagram of a Nine-Patch block. Notice where the small squares are

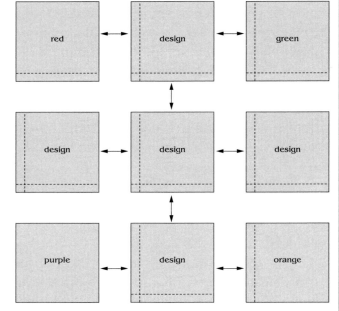

DIAGRAM 10-8

Looking at the right side of the Nine-Patch block, the dotted lines represent the ¼" seam allowance lines drawn on the back of each square.

The squares are first sewn into rows, then the rows are joined to form a block.

joined to each other. With careful planning, you can save a great deal of time by marking only the lines that will actually be sewn (Diagram 10-8).

If you follow the suggested arrangement of the squares for your Nine-Patch design, some squares require only one seam allowance, some require two, and some require none at all.

For the Flavor Quilt, all seam allowances are ¼" from the raw edge of the fabric, and marked with a sharp #2 pencil on the back or wrong side of the fabric. Be sure to mark the lines accurately, otherwise your quilt blocks will not all be the same size and the quilt will not fit together properly.

If you have cut your squares using the strip method and rotary cutter, you will already have one seam line drawn. Here's the rest of the formula. (Remember, all the seam lines are on the wrong side, or back of the fabric.)

- The red-dyed squares in the upper left corner need one seam line, on the bottom edge. When the top row is stitched together, this line will join with the lines on the other two squares in the row to form a seam line to join the top row to the middle row.

- The green-dyed squares in the upper right corner need two seam lines, one on the bottom edge, and one on the side that joins the middle square. These two lines are on the wrong side of the fabric. When you hold the right side of the square up to the light, the two seam lines should make the letter "L" through the fabric.

- All of the crayon squares should have a similar "L" marked on the back. Although you don't always need two lines, you won't know which crayon squares will be sewn into which position until after the designs have been ironed onto the fabric. It's easier just to mark all the squares the same way.

- The purple-dyed square in the bottom left corner doesn't need any seam lines. It will be stitched using the seam lines on the middle crayon square in the bottom row.
- The orange-dyed square in the bottom right corner needs one seam line, on the side that joins it to the middle square.
- All of the short lattice strips in the Large Flavor Quilt need seam allowance lines on both long edges of each strip.
- The large crayon blocks don't need any seam lines. The short lattice strips that join the large blocks to the Nine-Patch blocks have the seam lines.
- The long lattice strips and the borders don't need seam lines. These will be sewn by machine, using the edge of the presser foot as the ¼" guide.
- Mark all the appropriate seam lines on the fabric before assembling the quilt. The small squares already have one seam line. Add the second seam line while watching television or talking on the phone, working on a lap board.

IRONING QUILT BLOCKS

Quilt seams are usually ironed to one side, rather than being pressed open. Use plenty of steam and iron from the right side of the fabric, to make sure the seam is pressed completely flat, without any pleats at the seamline.

Wherever seams meet at a corner, it's a good idea to press them in opposite directions, to avoid a large lump of fabric. To do this in a Nine-Patch, iron the top and bottom rows with the seams pointing to the left, and the middle row with the seams pointing to the right. Read the section on assembling the Nine-Patch block in the Large Flavor Quilt chapter for more detailed instructions.

Avoid making heavy seams fold back on themselves. Wherever possible, iron finished blocks flat, with the seams pressed into the lattice strips. The quilt top will be much smoother.

Avoid distorting your quilt blocks when ironing. It's a good idea to use the flat edge of the iron, rather than the point, when pressing seams. Too much pressure with the point of a hot steam iron can curve the fabric.

EVERYTHING ELSE
YOU WANTED TO KNOW

Complete, step-by-step instructions for making the Flavor Quilt are in the chapter of the same name. Many other types of quilts can be made the same way: first assemble the blocks, then add the joining or "lattice" strips, sew the borders and complete the quilt top. Follow the directions in the Flavor Quilt chapter for hints on sewing, measuring and assembling the top.

Instructions for making the quilt backing, layering the quilt "sandwich," pin basting and machine quilting are also given in that chapter. Though the directions refer specifically to the Flavor Quilt, the same process is used for many other types of quilts. Binding and finishing the quilt are also covered.

Refer to the Sources & Resources chapter for suggested reading to help you learn more about quiltmaking.

Making A Miniature Flavor Quilt

Finished size: 8" x 8"

Creating a miniature Flavor Quilt is a good way to teach children simple surface design and sewing. The pattern is a basic Nine-Patch block, with all the stitching on straight lines.

Given supervision, children from second grade on can do all the work themselves. Younger children will require adult help, although most preschool and kindergarten kids can sew remarkably well – if you give them enough time and encouragement.

Here is a small project you can do with your own children, working on it a little at a time, or finishing the whole thing in one session.

As a group project (class, school, club, etc.), miniature quilts can be created in a single, all-day workshop, or over a period of several days or weeks.

I use the miniature format in half-day workshops for museums, schools and art guilds. Each child in the workshop must come with an older helper, and each adult/child team creates a single miniature quilt. I love it when fathers come too!

A miniature quilt is also an excellent way to teach the Flavor Quilt project to adults in a half-day workshop. All the techniques can be discussed, and many explored, giving the adults not only a completed miniature quilt for a sample, but also the expertise they need to teach the project to others. It's a good workshop for teachers, club leaders, therapists, etc. Adults have just as much fun as the little kids when they work with the paint!

Since it takes more than half a day to dye fabric in powdered soft drink mix, I dye a set of squares before class, packing one of each color in the miniature kits. Sometimes I do a dyeing demonstration during the workshop; sometimes I have participants dye extra muslin squares, leaving the process for me to finish later.

Before attempting this project, read through all the other chapters of this book that refer to the process you plan to use

MATERIALS

For each miniature quilt, you will need:

- Four 3" squares of prewashed, unbleached, unmercerized 100% cotton muslin (read about fabric in the chapter on dyeing with powdered soft drink mix; read about cutting and marking fabric in the Basic Quilting chapter)
- Five 3" squares of prewashed white polyester/cotton fabric (read about fabric in the chapter on fabric crayons)
- One 9½" square of white poly/cotton fabric for the back
- One 7½" square of batting
- A resealable plastic sandwich bag to keep it all in
- Powdered soft drink mix and equipment for dyeing (see the Dyeing chapter for details)
- Fabric crayons, paper, dye sticks, fabric paint, permanent pens (read the chapters that deal with these materials first)
- Needles, pins, thread, scissors (read the Sewing chapter)

METHOD

- Using a sharp pencil, draw ¼" seam allowances on two edges of each 3" square to form the letter "L." An adult should do this, to make sure the seams are accurate. (Diagram 11-1)

- Dye the four unmercerized muslin squares in powdered soft drink mix, following the instructions in the Dyeing chapter of this book.

- Use fabric crayons, dye sticks or paint to decorate the five small poly/cotton squares. Refer to the appropriate sections of this book for specific instructions. Keep the design in the center of each square; the edges will be used for seam allowance. Be sure to decorate the plain side of each square. Looking at the right (unmarked) side of the fabric, the seam allowance lines should be on the wrong side of the fabric on the left and bottom edges. Hold your square up to the light and you should see the letter "L" through the fabric. (Diagram 11-2)

- Decorate the large square for the back of the quilt, using handprints, crayons, tie dye, stamps, etc. Keep your design in the center of the square, since the edges will be rolled over for binding.

- When all fabric has been dyed or decorated, dried and heat-set, you are ready to assemble the miniature quilt.

- Line up the Nine-Patch in three rows of three squares, arranging the plain dyed squares and the decorated squares in a pleasing design. It's like playing tic-tac-toe. Try to put the nicest design in the center, since this will be the focus. (Diagram 11-3)

- Check the seam allowance lines on the back of each square. When you hold the square up to the light, the seam allowance lines should make the letter "L." Add new seam allowances to decorated blocks, if necessary.

- Starting with the top row, pin the middle square to the left-hand square, right sides together, matching edges carefully. Place the pin directly beneath the line to be sewn, pointing in the direction the child will sew. (Diagram 11-4)

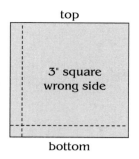

DIAGRAM 11-1
Mark ¼" seam allowance in "L" shape on wrong side of fabric.

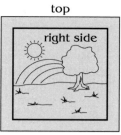

DIAGRAM 11-2
Front of decorated 3" square.

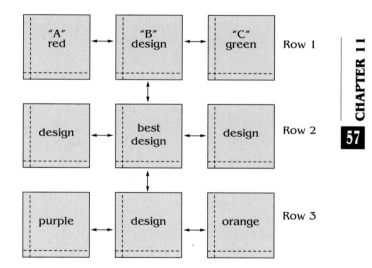

DIAGRAM 11-3
Arrange the Nine-Patch block with the seam allowances on the back (dotted lines) forming the letter "L."

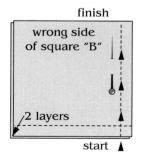

DIAGRAM 11-4
Pin square "A" to square "B," right sides together. Place the pin under the line to be sewn, pointing in the direction to be sewn.

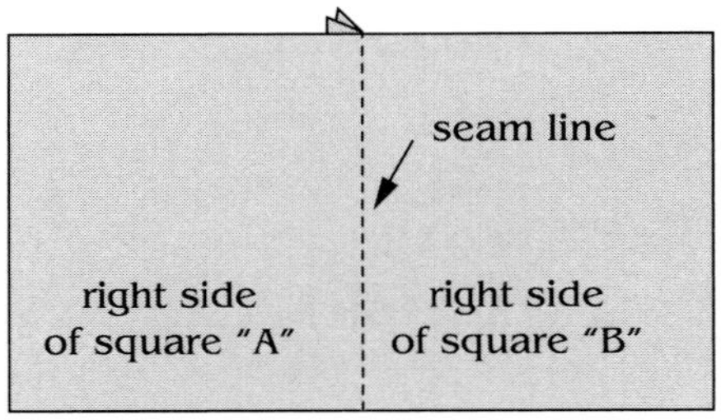

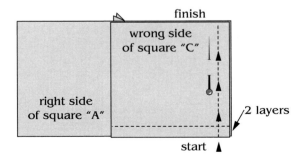

DIAGRAM 11-5
When stitched together, the first two squares open like a book.

DIAGRAM 11-6
Pin square "C" to square "B", right sides together. Sew to complete row 1.

- Thread a needle (#7 Sharps or #9 Crewel needles have nice big eyes and are small enough for little hands to hold) with a good quality thread (inexpensive polyester tangles too easily). Pull the thread through the eye until you have a double length of about 14". Knot the two ends together so the thread won't pull out of the fabric or the needle.

- Starting at the right hand edge of the fabric, sew a running stitch exactly on the line, from right to left (refer to Diagram 11-4). (This will be reversed for left-handers.) Be sure to make the stitches as small as possible, and keep them exactly on the line. Make sure the two pieces of fabric stay in alignment; the back piece often slips when the child is not looking. Teach the child that one stitch goes in AND out, not in and pull through to the back, then push back to the front (stab stitch). Since the seam line is on the front, the child has no way of finding where to put the needle on the back. Often, the child will "jump" over the raw edge, back to the front, making a whip stitch instead of a running stitch. Only the tip of the needle is pushed into the fabric, then brought back out to the front. If the child pushes most of the needle into the fabric, a huge stitch or "toe catcher" will be made. Do not remove the pin until the two pieces have been sewn together. Finish the seam by overcasting, making three stitches, all in the same space, and on the line.

- Open the two squares like a book. Check to make sure the stitches caught both pieces of fabric. Make sure there's no "air conditioning" (gaps) in the seam (Diagram 11-5).

- Pin the third square in the top row to the middle square, right sides together. Stitch as before (Diagram 11-6). Set the finished row of three aside.

- Pin and sew the middle and bottom rows the same way.
- When all three rows are sewn, press the seams of each row in opposite directions. Press the top and bottom row seams towards the left hand side, and the middle row seams to the right hand side. This eliminates bulk when you sew the rows together. It's really hard for a child to stitch through six layers of fabric!
- Pin the top and middle rows together, being careful to match corners (seams should be in opposite directions). Sew along the seam line. Be sure to stitch through the bulky seams (Diagram 11-7).
- Pin and sew the bottom row to the middle row.
- Check the Nine-Patch for missed stitches, then steam press from the right side, ironing the row-joining seams in one direction.
- Iron the backing square. Lay the backing square WRONG side up, center the batting on it, then center the Nine-Patch on the batting. Be sure the "top" edge of your backing square corresponds to the "top" edge of the Nine-Patch, so that all the designs appear the right way up. Pin the layers together (Diagram 11-8).
- Doing one side at a time, fold the raw edges of the backing square over about ¼", then fold again to cover ¼" of the raw edges of the Nine-Patch. Pin, then sew, using either a running stitch or a small whip stitch. Fold all four edges the same way, squaring off the corners. Be sure to sew right at the fold where it touches the Nine-Patch, or the edges will come loose (Diagram 11-9).
- You can finish the miniature quilt by tying the four corners of the center square with yarn, or by quilting around the designs. Children have a hard time with quilting stitches, especially if the crayons or dye sticks have made the fabric stiff. If you

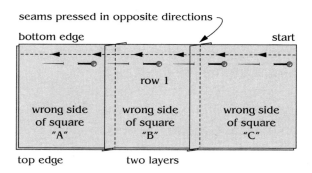

DIAGRAM 11-7
Pin row 1 to row 2, right sides together. Sew across seam line.

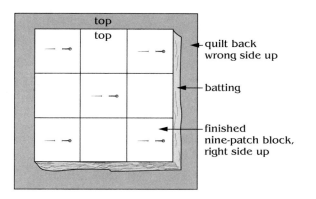

DIAGRAM 11-8
Assemble the three layers of the quilt.

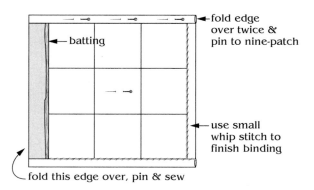

DIAGRAM 11-9

have used polyester batting, the miniature quilt really doesn't need quilting.

- Don't forget to sign and date the quilt with a permanent fabric pen.
- Sew small fabric loops or plastic rings to the edge or back of the quilt for hanging. It's fun to suspend the quilt so both sides can be seen. Don't display the quilt in direct sunlight or it will fade.

IS IT A POT HOLDER?

Show a group of children a miniature quilt and ten children out of ten will triumphantly tell you that it's a pot holder! Practical souls, they are delighted to make something useful. In their reckoning, a pot holder has more value than a miniature quilt. An alarming number of adults have this same opinion.

I have a personal bias against hand made pot holders: why waste valuable time making something that will be covered with gravy spills, burns and grease spots? Remember that the powdered soft drink dye is not very washable. In addition, polyester batting is dangerous when heated (it burns easily and melts to create potential skin burn hazards).

A little education is needed. Is a quilt art? Check out the high prices collectors pay for antique quilts. Look in any museum or art gallery for their quilt collections. Dozens of corporations have large quilt collections hanging in their offices.

While a child's miniature quilt may not be worth a fortune in money, it's a priceless keepsake for family members. Add it to your family's own personal treasures. Treat it with respect. When the child is an adult that little square of drawings, paint, handprints and stitches will hold a bundle of special memories.

The Large Flavor Quilt

A GROUP QUILT PROJECT FOR 100 CHILDREN
Finished size: 82" x 57"

The Flavor Quilt is a large wallhanging with twenty Nine-Patch blocks and twenty plain blocks. These square blocks are decorated with fabric crayons, and measure 7¾" each before sewing. Lattice strips, 1½" wide, are used between the blocks and the rows. The handprint borders are 8" wide, with a dedication block in the top center. Quarter-inch finished binding matches the lattice. The quilt back is either pieced fabric, or a twin-sized sheet. Thin, machine-type polyester batting is used inside, and the hanging has minimal machine quilting with invisible nylon thread. A sleeve is attached to the back of the quilt for hanging.

EQUIPMENT AND SUPPLIES
- Unsweetened powdered soft drink mix (4 packages each of red, orange, purple, green)
- 1 cup table salt
- 4 plastic containers (one gallon size)
- 4 wooden spoons
- 4 quarts boiling water

- 5-10 packages of fabric crayons
- 2-3 extra fine point black permanent marking pens
- 150, 2¾" squares of paper (typing or copy machine weight)
- 25, 7¾" squares paper (typing or copy machine weight)
- 10 sheets white paper (for ironing)
- 25 #2 pencils with erasers (one per child in each class)

- Plastic baskets or containers to hold crayons

- Fabric paint (1 small jar of red, yellow, blue)
- 3 plastic plates with ½" thick fine-textured sponge cut to fit (one plate for each color)
- Newspapers
- Paper towels and soap, sink and running water

- 1 old dry iron for crayons
- 1 steam iron for sewing
- Old sheet, folded for ironing pad
- Large and small recloseable plastic bags for storage

SEWING SUPPLIES
- 1 pkg. colored ball-headed pins
- 2 pkg. easy-to-thread sewing needles (#7 Sharps, #9 Crewel, or round-eyed sewing needles, not craft or darning needles)
- 5 spools good quality thread (natural, white or gray)
- 5 pairs sharp children's scissors
- 5 pincushions
- 5 baskets or containers to hold sewing supplies

- Sewing thread to finish quilt (gray or natural, and color to match quilt backing and binding)
- Smoke nylon thread for machine quilting
- 400 large safety pins for basting (1"-2" size)
- 8 large Bulldog or binder clips (for basting)

- Purple disappearing quilt marking pen (NOT the kind you have to wash out)
- Sewing machine

FABRIC REQUIREMENTS

First read the information about fabric in the chapters on dyeing with powdered soft drink mix and working with crayons and paints. Make sure all fabric has been washed and ironed before cutting. Do not use bleach or fabric softener, or detergents containing these products.

- 1 yard 100% cotton untreated muslin for dyeing with soft drink mix
- 2¼ yards 42-44" wide polyester/cotton blend for crayons (at least 65% polyester or more)
- ¾ yard 90" or 108" wide 100% cotton bleached muslin for handprint borders (or 1⅔ yards 42-44" wide bleached muslin)
- 1⅓ yards 42-44" wide 100% cotton, small print or color of choice (for lattice strips and binding)
- 4 yards 42-44" wide 100% cotton print or one flat twin sized sheet (for back of quilt)
- Thin quilt batting, twin size or at least 60" x 85"

CUTTING AND MARKING THE QUILT

First read about marking fabric and using a rotary cutter, cutting strips and cutting multiple squares in the Basic Quilting chapter.

DYED SQUARES

You will need 80 squares for the quilt, but cut at least 100 squares (or one for each child). Look in the Basic Quilting chapter for diagrams illustrating the cutting and marking of strips and squares

- Rip one end of the prewashed muslin to get the straight cross grain. With right sides together, fold the fabric in half, along the lengthwise grain, selvage to selvage, matching the ripped edges exactly. Iron, using plenty of steam and creasing the fold. (Don't worry if you can't tell which is the right side. The side with the seam lines will become the "wrong" side.)
- Using a rotary cutter and a large plastic quilting ruler, trim off the ripped edge.
- With a sharp #2 pencil, mark ¼" seam allowance on one side of the cut edge of fabric.
- Using a rotary cutter and large plastic quilting ruler, cut one 3" strip, measuring from the cut edge.
- Turn the strip over and mark the ¼" seam allowance on the matching edge. (When your strip is opened up, there should be one continuous line along one edge.)
- Repeat the marking and cutting process until you have nine strips, each 3" wide.
- Stack the strips carefully into three sets, three strips in each, all selvage ends together. Using the horizontal lines on your ruler, make a right angle cut, trimming off the selvage ends.
- Cut the stacks into 3" squares. You should get at least six stacks of squares from each set of strips, at least 108 squares (Diagram 12-1).
- Mark the ¼" seam allowance on one other edge of each square to make the letter "L".
- Separate the marked squares into stacks of 25 and store in four sealed plastic bags, one set for each color. Keep the extras for emergencies.

SMALL CRAYON SQUARES

You will need 100 small squares for the Nine-Patch blocks, plus at least ten extra for "mistakes" or "test runs."

Assuming that your polyester blend fabric will shrivel under the hot iron, a slight adjustment in cutting size should take care of the loss. Cut the squares 3⅛" and they should shrink to 3" after the crayons are transferred. If the crayon transfer process does not diminish the size of your fabric, cut to the 3" size to start with. The 7¾" squares should always be trimmed down to size after the transfer process, regardless of shrinkage, to give them an accurate edge.

- Rip, fold and iron polyester/cotton fabric in the same way as the dyed fabric. Trim edge and mark ¼" seam allowance as before. Refer to the "Basic Quilting" chapter for cutting and marking directions and diagrams.
- Cut nine strips, each 3⅛" wide. After each strip is cut, turn it and mark ¼" seam allowance on the back.
- Stack strips into three sets of three, all selvages even. Trim selvages, using the horizontal lines of your ruler to make a right angle cut.
- Cut 3⅛" squares. You should get six or seven stacks from each strip set, depending on the width of your fabric.
- Mark a second ¼" seam on each square to make an "L," as before. You should have about 126 squares.
- Store marked squares in recloseable plastic bag.

LARGE CRAYON SQUARES

You will need 20 large crayon squares for the body of the quilt plus one extra for the dedication block in the top border.

The squares are cut slightly larger than needed, and trimmed back to the finished 7¾" size for greater accuracy.

- Rip one end of the remaining polyester/cotton fabric on the cross grain.
- Accurately measure 8" below the ripped edge, snip with scissors and rip an 8" strip across the width of the fabric. Check to make sure the entire strip is 8" wide. If it is not, you will have to cut your strips.

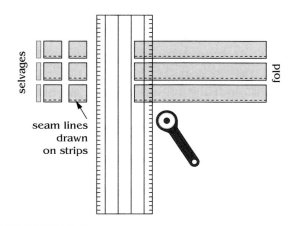

DIAGRAM 12-1
Stack strips into three sets, then cut into squares.

- Repeat the ripping process, measuring each strip in turn, until you have five 8" strips, each 42-44" long.
- Carefully stack strips (do not fold) and recut into 8" squares. You should get 25 squares. Refer to the Basic Quilting chapter for cutting directions and diagrams.
- Check to make sure squares have no wrinkles or loose threads that will interfere with the crayon transfers. Store flat in a large recloseable plastic bag.
- Use any leftover fabric to cut extra 3⅛" squares.

NOTE: You do not need to mark seam allowances on 8" squares.

LATTICE STRIPS

All lattice strips are cut 1½" wide. You will need 35 short strips, 7¾" long, to join the blocks; 6 long strips, approximately 66", to join the rows; and two side strips approximately 43", depending on your row measurements.

NOTE: The exact length of the long lattice strips depends on the average length of the rows. This measurement may vary up to two inches from quilt to quilt, and can only be determined after the blocks are joined into rows. Do not cut the long lattice strips into lengths until you have this figure.

- Rip edge of lattice fabric on the cross grain. Fold fabric in half, right sides together, selvage to selvage on the lengthwise grain, precisely matching the ripped crossgrain edge. Don't worry if the selvages are not straight – it's the cross grain that's important. Iron, creasing the fold. Refer to the Basic Quilting chapter for diagrams.
- Trim the ripped edge with your rotary cutter. Mark a seam line ¼" from the trimmed edge with a sharp #2 pencil. Carefully measure 1" from the first line and draw a second line on the fabric.

- Using the trimmed edge and the horizontal lines on your ruler as a guide, cut a 1½" wide strip. Turn the strip over and mark seam lines on the other half of the strip. The seams should be ¼" from each cut edge (Diagram 12-2).
- Repeat the marking and cutting process until you have seven strips.
- Fold the remaining fabric on the lengthwise grain to form four layers, carefully matching the cut edges. Iron, creasing the fold. Pin the cut edge on the remaining fabric to hold the layers in place, and set aside.
- Carefully stack the seven marked strips with all selvage ends together into two sets, one with three folded strips, one with four. Line the two stacks up, side by side (Diagram 12-3).
- Trim off selvages, using horizontal lines on your ruler to make a right angle cut. Measure and cut strips into 7¾" lengths. The final pieces will be cut by opening the fold.
- You should have 35 pieces, 1½" x 7¾", marked with ¼" seam allowance lines on the wrong side of all 7¾" edges. (There will be two seam lines drawn on each strip.) Store in small, recloseable plastic bag.
- Put the remaining lattice fabric (now folded in four layers) back on your cutting board, carefully remove the pins and check the cut edge for accuracy. Trim, if necessary.
- Cut 12 strips, 1½" wide, for the long lattice that joins row to row, and the shorter side pieces. Pin the cut edge of the remaining fabric and set aside.
- Remove the selvages on the cut strips, then use a matching thread and very small stitches to machine sew the 12 strips together into one long strip. Steam press the seams open.
- Set this long piece aside until you are

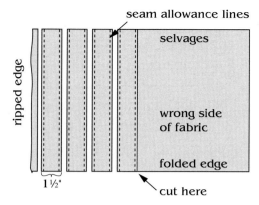

DIAGRAM 12-2
Mark ¼" seam allowances and cut 1½" wide strips.

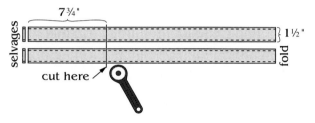

DIAGRAM 12-3
Line up strips in two stacks; trim selvages, then cut into 7¾" lengths.

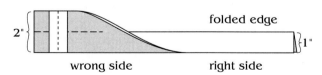

DIAGRAM 12-4
Press 2" wide binding strip in half to make 1" wide double strip.

ready to join the rows of the quilt together.

BINDING

You will need at least 280" (approximately 8 yards) of binding for your quilt.

Although bed quilts are traditionally bound with fabric cut on the bias (to improve wear), a wallhanging can be bound with a simple cross grain binding, cut as strips. The double-fold binding provides a sturdy edge.

- Put the remaining lattice fabric on your cutting board, remove the pins and check the cut edge for accuracy. Trim if necessary.
- Cut seven strips 2" wide.
- Remove the selvages, then use matching thread and very small stitches to machine sew the seven strips together into one long piece.
- Press all seams open. Fold the strip in half, lengthwise, to make a 1" double strip (Diagram 12-4). Steam press the full length of the fabric. Set the binding aside until needed.

BORDERS

The four borders are 8" wide. The two long borders are cut 87" long, and finish to approximately 83"; the two short borders are cut 46" long, and finish to approximately 42½".

NOTE: You cannot determine the precise border lengths until you measure the finished center of the quilt top. The measurements given allow several inches of "fudge" room.

- Rip one edge of border fabric on the cross grain, from selvage to selvage.
- Accurately measure 8" from the ripped edge, snip with scissors and rip a strip across the width of the fabric. Measure at several points along the length of the strip to make sure it is all 8" wide. (If it

does not rip straight, you will have to cut your strips.)

- You will need three strips if you are using 90" or 108" wide fabric; seven strips if you are using 42-44" wide fabric.
- Make a right angle cut on the end of each strip, removing the selvage.
- Using matching thread and very small stitches, machine sew the strips into one long piece. Steam press the whole strip, ironing the seams open.
- Cut two long borders 87". Find the center of each border by folding each strip in half. Mark the center with a small pencil dot on the edge of the fabric, right at the fold. Leaving the fabric folded in half, measure 41½" from the fold towards the ends, and mark all the edges with a pencil as before. The fabric between the pencil mark and the end of the strip is your "fudge" room. Be sure no handprints or names appear in this area, because they may be cut off later.
- On the top border, mark 4" either side of the center line. This is where the quilt dedication block will go. Do not put any handprints or names in this area. (Diagram 12-5)
- Cut two short borders 46". Find the center of each border and mark, as before. With borders still folded, measure 21¼" from the center line, and mark all layers.
- Carefully check all borders and remove creases and loose threads that would interfere with printing.
- Fold borders neatly and store in large, recloseable plastic bag.

QUILT BACKING

An inexpensive, flat twin sized sheet is often the cheapest way to back the quilt. Since the hanging will be machine quilted, the tightly-woven sheet fabric will not be a problem. I do not recommend using sheets for quilts that will be finished by hand. It's

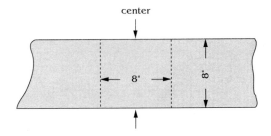

DIAGRAM 12-5
Mark top border for dedication block. Do not place handprints in this area.

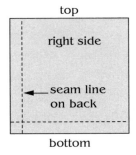

DIAGRAM 12-6
Place fabric square right side up with seam lines forming the letter "L" on the back.

very hard to hand quilt through the tightly woven sheet fabric.

The sheet should be washed and ironed. You may wish to remove the stitching and fold out the hems to allow more fabric. Most sheets are sewn with a chain-stitch; if you find the correct direction, you can cut a single stitch and then pull all the remaining stitches free in a flash! Nothing more needs to be done to the sheet – it's already the right size for the quilt backing.

If you are using four yards of fabric for the quilt back, you will need to sew a center seam to make it wide enough. Bed quilts are traditionally backed with fabric cut into three segments in order to avoid a center seam that can create a ridge. This center ridge can wear out faster than the rest of the quilt. A backing with two seams is also stronger than one with a single seam; less stress is placed on the stitches. Since we are making a wallhanging, we can use a center seam without worrying about wear and tear.

It's important to choose a backing fabric with a busy, overall print that will hide the seam and any less-than-perfect stitches or small ripples in the machine quilting.

Be sure your fabric is not a stripe, diagonal, plaid, or one-way design. These are hard to join accurately, and there is no yardage allowance for matching patterns.

• Wash and iron the fabric. Fold and cut into two equal pieces, each 2 yards long and about 44" wide.

• Snip and rip off the selvage from the inside edges of each piece. If your fabric has a "one way" design, be sure the pattern is pointing "up" on both pieces.

• Using matching thread and a fairly small stitch length, machine sew the two pieces together, carefully matching the ends.

• Press the seam to one side, ironing from the right side of the fabric to avoid pleats

and tucks. Pressing the seam to one side makes a stronger join after the hanging is quilted. If you press the seam open, only the thread in your stitches holds the two pieces together.

• Set backing aside until needed.

ARTWORK FOR THE FLAVOR QUILT

Before your quilt group's first session, read the chapters on working with children, dyeing with powdered soft drink mix, working with fabric paint and fabric crayons.

With a group of 100 children, it's easiest to divide into four sessions, with 25 children in each session. Be sure you have enough adult helpers, especially if you're working with young children.

DYED SQUARES

Follow chapter directions, dyeing at least 20 squares of four different colors for a total of 80 dyed squares. Let each child dye at least one square. Remind them that they will not get their particular square back (kids can be very possessive) – they will be dyeing fabric for everyone to use in the quilt.

SMALL CRAYON SQUARES

Have each child produce at least one small crayon square on the 2¾" paper. The drawings should completely fill the paper, with no white space around the edges. Follow instructions in the chapter about crayons for transferring the best designs onto cloth, and proceed as follows.

• Place your white fabric square right side up on a clean piece of paper on the ironing surface. The seam allowance lines should be on the underside of the fabric on the left edge and the bottom edge. If you hold the fabric up to the light, the two seam lines should make the letter "L" through the fabric (Diagram 12-6).

• Carefully position a crayon square, color

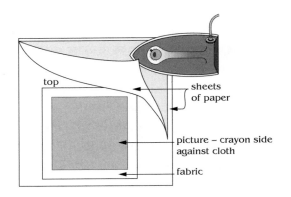

top

sheets
of paper

picture – crayon side
against cloth

fabric

DIAGRAM 12-7
*Position crayon drawing on right side of cloth,
fitting the picture into the "L." Press between two
sheets of white paper to transfer the image.*

side against the fabric, so that the paper fits into the corner of the "L", leaving about ¼" white seam allowance all around the edge. Be sure that the top of the drawing corresponds to the top of the fabric square (Diagram 12-7).

• Cover with a clean sheet of paper and iron, following directions in the Crayon chapter.

• Repeat this process until you have at least 100 small squares, all with seam lines making an "L" on the back. It is not necessary to change the paper on the ironing pad after each small transfer operation. Move to a clean area of paper, and change only when the paper becomes discolored. After a few transfers, the paper will be quite hot, and the transfer process will take only a few seconds. Be sure to work on a hard surface and press down hard with the iron to get brilliant colors.

• Outline the crayon designs with an extra fine point permanent black marker, following the original pencil lines.

• Choose the 20 best pictures – these will go in the center of each Nine-Patch. Find 40 pictures that match well with your center squares – these will finish off the center row of the Nine-Patch blocks.

LARGE CRAYON SQUARES

Divide your groups of 25 children into five teams (five children in each team). Let each team decide on a design idea for a block. Each team produces one large crayon drawing on paper, which is then transferred onto cloth and outlined. You will need 20 of these large squares, five from each of your four classes.

Use a large quilt ruler or square and rotary cutter to trim each finished fabric block to exactly 7¾" square.

DEDICATION BLOCK

Assign a person (possibly the art teacher) or group to produce the dedication block, which will be sewn into the upper border. The block should say where the quilt was made, when and why, with appropriate artwork. For instance, it could say, "The Charlotte's Web Quilt, made by Third Grade students at Nursery Road Elementary School," and then the city and date, with pictures of Charlotte and Wilbur in the background. Do not trim this block until you are ready to assemble the border.

HANDPRINT BORDERS

Read the chapter on working with fabric paint and doing handprints. Cover a long table with newspaper and set one border strip at a time on the table. Be sure the borders are right side up, and that all creases and loose threads have been removed from the surface.

Have everybody in the quilt project make an autographed handprint on the borders, spacing or overlapping hands, depending on the number and size of the hands.

Note: Be sure that handprints and names do not extend into areas that will be cut off, or sewn into seams! The ends of the borders will be trimmed, as will the center panel of the top border. The edges of the borders will be stitched into the quilt (at least ¼" will be lost on each side).

**ASSEMBLING THE
NINE-PATCH QUILT BLOCKS**

A Nine-Patch block looks like tic-tac-toe: it's one of the simplest blocks, very easy to construct because it's all straight lines (refer to Diagram 10-8, page 54).

Each of the 20 blocks will be assembled the same way. Refer to the diagrams in Chapter 11 for Nine-Patch assembly. Start by sewing the upper left square to the middle square to make two pieces that

open like a book. Then add the upper right square so you have a row.

Repeat the same sequence with the middle row, and then the bottom row. Then join row to row, and you will have your block!

Before you meet with the quilt group, prepare all your materials. Make sure that all the artwork has been properly outlined and heat-set, and that the dyed soft drink blocks have been steam pressed into shape. Check to make sure all the seam lines are drawn on the back of each square, and that the lines are in the correct position. Read the chapters on Teaching Children to Sew and Making a Miniature Flavor Quilt. These will tell you how to set up the sewing room and prepare the blocks to be sewn.

Decide on the arrangement of the dyed squares. I usually put them in the four corners, red and green in the top row, purple and orange in the bottom row.

The best-looking drawings go in the center of the block, with the next-best on either side. The weaker drawings go in the top and bottom rows, between the dyed squares.

Lay out your 20 Nine-Patch blocks, making sure that all the seam lines are underneath, forming the letter "L" (add new seam allowances, if necessary), then pin as follows. (Refer to the diagrams in Chapter 11.)

• Starting with the top row, pin the upper left (red) square to the middle square in the top row, right sides together, matching edges. Be sure you place the pin directly beneath the line that is to be sewn, pointing in the direction the child will sew (refer to Chapter 9 on Teaching Children to Sew). Set the green square aside.

• Next, pin the middle row, pinning the drawing on the left to the center drawing in the same way. Use a black permanent pen to mark a small number "1" in the seam allowance. Write another small "1" in the seam allowance of the remaining piece in the row, then set it aside. If you code your center rows by number, you can quickly find the correct piece for each block.

• Use the same procedure to pin the purple square to the middle design in the bottom row, setting the orange square aside.

• Repeat this pinning process for all 20 of the Nine-Patch blocks, using code numbers one through twenty on the center rows for quick matching.

Now you're ready to thread at least 25 needles. Put five threaded needles in each pincushion, then put the pincushion, thread, scissors and needle-threader in a basket – one for each sewing group.

SEWING THE NINE-PATCH BLOCKS

At the beginning of each group sewing session, explain exactly what you want your children to do (refer to Chapter 9 for a sample lecture). Explain how a Nine-Patch block is sewn, showing examples of each step in construction. Demonstrate the running stitch to each child.

When the stitched pairs are finished, pin the appropriate third square to the middle square of each, being sure the seam lines are in the correct position and that the pin is directly below the line to be sewn, pointing in the right direction.

After the three squares are stitched into rows, each row must be ironed before it can be joined to another row.

To avoid stitching through six layers of fabric where the center seams come together, those seams should be pressed in opposite directions.

Using a steam iron (make sure it doesn't spit or drip on the soft drink squares, or they will be stained) and iron-

ing on the right side of the fabric, press the seams in the top and bottom rows towards the left. Press the seams in all the middle rows towards the right (refer to Diagram 11-7, page 59). Be careful not to make any pleats or tucks as you iron. Each seam should be ironed completely flat.

A quick trick for ironing if you're right handed: turn all the middle rows upside down, with the right side of the fabric still facing you. You can then iron all three rows with the seams to the left, yet when the middle rows are turned around, they'll have seams pointing to the right! Saves trying to iron left to right, which is very awkward.

You are now ready to pin the rows. If you have placed your seam lines in the proper position, each row should have a continuous line across the bottom, on the wrong side.

Pin the top row to the center row by first placing right sides together and matching the center seams exactly. You should have seams on the top row facing to the left, seams on the middle row facing to the right. These opposing seams should butt neatly together, making a perfect join. Place four pins across the row, directly beneath the line to be sewn and pointing from right to left (Refer to Diagram 11-7, page 59).

The row is now ready to be sewn straight across the seam line from one edge to the other. Remind your children to keep their running stitches small, and to make sure their stitches are going through all layers of fabric (especially hard at the seams where there is more fabric). Make sure they check for "air conditioning" where the seams come together.

Pin the bottom row to the middle row in the same way, and sew.

The finished Nine-Patch should be steam pressed on the right side of the fabric, with both long seams pointing towards the bottom of the block. Be sure, when you press, that there are no hidden tucks or pleats in the seam allowance. The block should be pressed completely flat.

With a square quilting ruler and rotary cutter, trim all the finished Nine-Patch blocks to precisely 7¾" square.

ASSEMBLING THE BLOCKS INTO ROWS

After the Nine-Patch blocks are sewn and trimmed, find a large area to lay out your quilt top (two large tables or a floor).

The Flavor Quilt has five rows, with eight blocks in each row. The blocks alternate, starting in the upper left corner with a Nine-Patch, followed by a team block, then a Nine-Patch, a team block and so on, ending the row with a team block. (Diagram 12-8)

Row two of the quilt starts with a team block and ends with a Nine-Patch. Rows three and five are the same as row one; row four matches row two.

Look at all of your blocks. Place the best-looking blocks in the most prominent position. Balance the colors. Yellow is especially dominant (though most quilts tend to look blue, because children use blue "sky" as a background). Try not to have blocks of the same dominant color too close to each other. If time allows, ask the children to help you arrange the blocks. Leave the blocks set up and come back later to look at them. If anything "leaps" out at you, move it to a better position.

When you are happy with the layout of your quilt, it's time to code each row and to pin the short lattice strips to each block.

Starting at the top of the quilt, code the blocks by row number and alphabetical position. The upper left corner block will be "1a," the next block "1b" and so on, with the final block in that row being "1h" (see diagram 12-8).

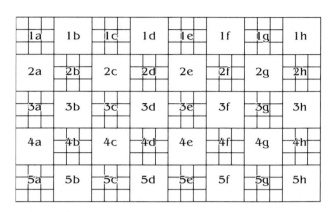

DIAGRAM 12-8
Placement and coding numbers for quilt blocks.

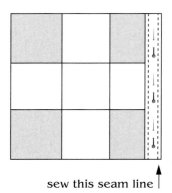

sew this seam line ↑

DIAGRAM 12-9
Pin lattice strips to right hand edge of blocks.

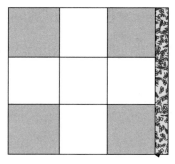

DIAGRAM 12-10
Press sewn lattice strip open with seam pointing into the lattice.

The next row begins "2a" and ends "2h." Be sure to use a permanent, extra fine point marker for this job, keeping the codes small and in the seam allowance in the middle of the top edge of each block. If you put the codes on the upper corners, they'll be stitched into the seam allowance and you won't be able to find them.

Next, carefully pin a 7¾" lattice strip to the right hand edge of every block except the "h" row – the final row on the right-hand side. Pin the strips to the blocks, right sides together, matching corners and edges accurately. Make sure the pins are beneath the seam line to be sewn, and pointing from right to left (Diagram 12-9).

Students can now sew the short lattice strips onto the blocks. Remember, it's the upper line only that will be sewn, the line that is ¼" from the raw edge of strip and block.

Remind students to keep their stitches small and not to pull their thread too tightly, or they will gather the fabric into pleats. As they sew, they should check to make sure the block fabric doesn't slip out of place behind the lattice strip.

After this first seam is sewn, press the lattice strip open, with the seam pointing into the lattice. Press from the right side of the fabric, making sure there are no pleats or tucks in the seam (Diagram 12-10).

Match the blocks into pairs, according to their codes (block "1a" should be pinned to block "1b," block "1c" to block "1d," etc.). Pin and sew in the same manner as before.

After the blocks are joined into pairs, press the seams into the lattice strips. Next, join a pair to a pair, following the correct code numbers and letters. Pin, sew and press as before. Continue in this manner until all eight blocks are joined into a row, and until all five rows have been assembled.

The quilt top is now completed, as far as the children are concerned. Set the rows out on a large table and arrange the borders in place, so everyone can admire the quilt.

The next step is to take the five rows and the borders, and assemble the final quilt by machine in your home or studio. If time and space allow, you could continue the assembly at school, with the children visiting from time to time to check your progress.

ASSEMBLING THE ROWS INTO A QUILT TOP

Measure every step of the way, and you'll have a quilt that hangs perfectly straight against a wall. No matter how the quilt blocks are put together by the children, finishing the top by machine guarantees a good-looking end product.

One hint to remember: Steam press from the right side after every seam is sewn. It's a good idea to keep your ironing board right beside your sewing machine.

If you treat the quilt top carefully, and don't wrinkle or bunch it as you sew, it should be perfectly smooth when all the pieces are joined. You'll be glad you did this – it's awfully hard to iron a quilt top with seams going in many different directions! If the top should need ironing before it's quilted, spot press any twisted seams from the back, but iron the entire top from the right side.

LONG LATTICE STRIPS

Start by ironing and then measuring each of the five quilt rows. Calculate the average length of the rows – your figure should be approximately 66", but this will vary, depending on the way the blocks were sewn.

Using your average measurement, cut

six lattice strips from the long 1½" wide piece. Save the remaining lattice.

Set out your quilt rows in correct order.

- Pin a lattice strip to the top edge of row 1, with right sides together, matching ends and easing any fullness. If the quilt row is shorter than the lattice, stretch it gently to fit. (Don't pull too hard, or you may pull out seams in the Nine-Patch blocks.) If you position your pins vertically to the edge of the fabric, you can carefully sew over them, or easily remove them as you stitch.

- With the lattice strip on the bottom, and using a gray or neutral colored thread and average stitch length, machine sew along the row, being careful not to "flip" any seams that you cross.

- Remove the pins and steam press from the right side, ironing the seam into the lattice. (This serves two purposes: the block seams will lie flat, and when you machine quilt "in the ditch," you will stitch through the blocks, thus holding them in position.)

- Pin a lattice strip to the bottom edge of row 1. Sew and press as before.

- Pin, sew and press lattice strips to the bottom edges of the remaining rows.

JOINING THE ROWS

The lattice strips in a quilt are really an optical illusion. The illusion created is that of an overall grid, like looking through a window with many panes of glass, and wood framing around each pane.

In reality, it is only the horizontal lines that are a complete strip. The vertical lines are made up of many short strips. To preserve this illusion, it is essential that the short strips line up exactly from top to bottom, giving the impression of a single piece of fabric. This requires careful pinning and sewing.

- With right sides together, and row 2 on

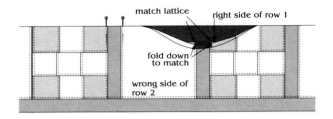

DIAGRAM 12-11
Fold back row 2 to match short lattice strips.

top, match the bottom edge of row 1's lattice strip to the top edge of row 2. You will be pinning from left to right, matching the ends.

- Since the long lattice strip of row 1 has no cross seams in it, there are no match points for row 2. To match the short lattice strips exactly, carefully fold back an inch of the top edge of row 2 at each cross-join as you come to it. Position the short lattice strips so that they match exactly. Without moving the join, fold row 2 back up to meet the top edge of row 1, and pin on both sides of the short lattice seams (Diagram 12-11).

- Continue matching and pinning all the cross seams. Match the ends of the rows.

- With row 1 on the bottom, machine stitch the rows together, being careful not to "flip" any seams that you cross.

- Remove all pins and steam press the seam from the right side, pressing the seam allowance into the lattice. Check to make sure that all your cross seams match perfectly.

- With row 3 on top, right sides together, pin the top of row 3 to the bottom of row 2, carefully matching cross seams. Sew and press as before. Again, check the cross seams to make sure the joins are making straight lines through the quilt.

- Repeat the process until the rows are all joined.

SEWING THE BORDERS

One of the biggest mistakes novice quilters make is in adding the borders. Many people cut a border strip much longer than they need, sew it to the quilt edge until they run out of quilt, and then cut off what's left of the border.

This is the perfect way to get wavy borders. Wavy, wobbly borders can be hidden when they're hanging over a bed, but a wall quilt must hang straight!

Why does the border ripple? Because a quilt top tends to grow slightly larger at the edges. Fabric stretches, seams may not be completely accurate. If you make a tiny error – say one sixty-fourth of an inch (about the width of a pencil line) – it may not seem very important. Make that same error on 64 pieces of fabric and suddenly you've added or subtracted a whole inch! Double the number of pieces and you have a two-inch error. It's hard to hide a problem that big!

Nobody can know exactly what your quilt top will measure until it's actually sewn. This is particularly true with quilts made by children, using many different sewing styles, not all of them especially accurate!

Sure, you can calculate what your quilt should be when it's finished, but those tiny differences in seam allowance can mean a loss or gain of several inches.

This is why you should never cut exact borders for a quilt before the quilt top is pieced. Forget what the magazines and pattern books say! Keep your border fabric separate – or add extra inches to the measurements – then cut your borders last to make your borders fit your quilt exactly.

The accurate measurement of your quilt top is through the center. To find the correct figures, fold your quilt top in half vertically, measuring along the fold to get the length of your quilt from top to bottom. Next, fold the quilt horizontally, measuring along the fold to get the width of your quilt. These are the correct figures for your borders (Diagram 12-12).

Before you add the borders to the Flavor Quilt, you need to sew the final lattice strips to the left and right (short) sides.

• Fold the quilt top in half, vertically. Carefully measure along the fold. Make sure the quilt is fully extended, but don't stretch the fabric. Write down this mea-

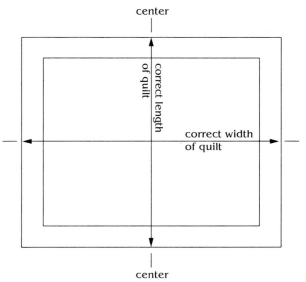

DIAGRAM 12-12
Fold quilt in half to get correct measurement for borders.

surement – it should be about 42 ½".

- Using this measurement, cut two lattice strips from the remaining 1½" fabric. Steam press the two short borders, then cut them the same length as the lattice, measuring from the center mark on each border strip. Be careful not to cut off any handprints or names.

- Pin a lattice strip to each side of the quilt top, working from edge to edge and easing fullness. With the lattice on the bottom, machine stitch the strip to the quilt, being careful not to "flip" any seams that you cross.

- Press the seam into the lattice, ironing from the right side.

- Pin a short border strip to each side of the quilt top, matching corners and easing any fullness. Be sure your handprints and names are pointing in the right direction, so they can be easily read when the quilt is on the wall.

- With the border fabric on the bottom, sew to the quilt. Steam press from the right side, ironing the seam into the lattice.

- Fold the quilt top in half, horizontally, matching the top and bottom edges. Measure along the fold, making sure that the quilt is fully extended. Do not stretch the fabric. The measurement should be approximately 82".

- Steam press the long borders. Cut the bottom border the correct length, measuring from the center mark.

- Using a large quilt ruler and rotary cutter, square up the sides of the dedication panel. Do not cut the top and bottom edges.

- Remove an 8" segment from the center of the top border, measuring from the center mark. Be sure to make right angle cuts.

- With matching thread and small stitches, machine sew the dedication block into

the center of the top border, matching it to the top and bottom edges of the border. Press the seams into the block.

- Fold the dedication block exactly in half and mark the center. Using this center mark as your guide, measure out towards the ends of the border and cut to the correct size.

- Fold the quilt top in half, vertically, matching upper left corner to upper right. Mark the center with a pin at the top and bottom edges.

- Match the exact center of the top border to the center of the quilt's top edge. Match the ends and edges, then pin the border to the quilt.

- With the border on the bottom, stitch it to the quilt, easing fullness. Steam press from the right side, ironing the seam into the lattice strip.

- Repeat this same process for the bottom border.

- Remove any stray threads from the outer surface of the quilt. Make sure no dark threads show through from the back. If you have ironed every step of the way, and treated the quilt top gently, it should not need any additional ironing. Steam press from the right side to remove any wrinkles – this is the last time the quilt will ever be ironed!

BASTING THE QUILT

Once the quilt top has been fully pieced, the three layers of the quilt must be basted together in preparation for quilting. Formerly, this basting was done by hand, using large needles and larger stitches. The thread was removed after quilting.

A faster way, and one that is preferred by machine quilters, is to use large safety pins to baste, instead of thread. The pins should be at least 1", and rustproof, since the powdered soft drink dye in the squares may cause the pins to tarnish.

A quilt of this size needs plenty of pins – a minimum of 400! The pins hold the three layers of fabric together while the quilt is being manhandled – or, more properly, womanhandled – through the sewing machine. After you have machine quilted a few hundred of these hangings, you may be able to work with fewer pins, relying on rolling the quilt layers and using your hands to keep the layers pucker-free.

When I was basting a quilt almost every week, I soon found that opening and closing 400 safety pins on a regular basis destroys both the skin and the feeling in your fingertips.

I now use 2" safety pins, which are much easier on the hands. They do, however, leave holes in the fabric, since they are made of much heavier wire. The holes can be rubbed or scratched away after the pins are removed, but it's a tedious business.

I leave my pins open when not in use. Saves time when I'm ready to baste!

LAYERING THE QUILT
- Measure the quilt top. It should be about 82" x 57".
- Make sure the backing fabric, or sheet, is much larger than the quilt top – at least 6" wider horizontally, and at least 12" longer, vertically. The batting should be about 3" larger than the top on all sides.
- Unfold two cardboard dressmaker's cutting boards onto a large table, or two tables pushed together. The top surface should be at least 85" long. Use Bulldog or binder clips to hold the two boards together.
- Iron the quilt backing, making sure that there are no loose dark threads that will show through the finished quilt.
- Spread the ironed backing, wrong side up, onto the cutting boards, extending

the long top edge, and the short left edge 2" over the edge of the cardboard. The bottom and right-hand edges of the back should hang freely over the edge of the cutting boards.
- Smooth the backing so that there are no wrinkles or puckers. Fold the extra fabric over to the back of the cardboard and clamp the fabric to the edges of the cutting boards with Bulldog clips.
- Open the batting, allowing it to "rest" if it has been tightly rolled. Spread the batting smoothly over the backing, allowing a 1" overhang on the top and left-hand edges. The bottom and right-hand edges should hang free. Without disturbing the backing, adjust the clamps to hold both backing and batting smoothly in place, folding the extra batting over to the back of the cardboard. Don't pull the batting or backing too tight or you will stretch it. Both will spring back into shape after you unclamp them, leaving the quilt wrinkled and puckered.
- Set the quilt top, right side up, onto the batting. The top and left-hand edges of the quilt top should be even with the edges of the cutting boards (no overlap). The bottom and right-hand edges of the quilt top should hang free. Smooth the quilt top until there are no wrinkles or puckers, then carefully remove the clamps and replace so that all three quilt layers are held smoothly in place.
- Check all edges of the quilt layers, to make sure there is enough fabric and batting. There should be extra backing fabric at the bottom of the quilt, and extra at the right-hand side, especially if a sheet has been used.
- Start pin-basting at the center of the quilt, working from the center towards the outer edges and smoothing the fabric layers as you go. Start by making a "plus" sign along the horizontal and vertical

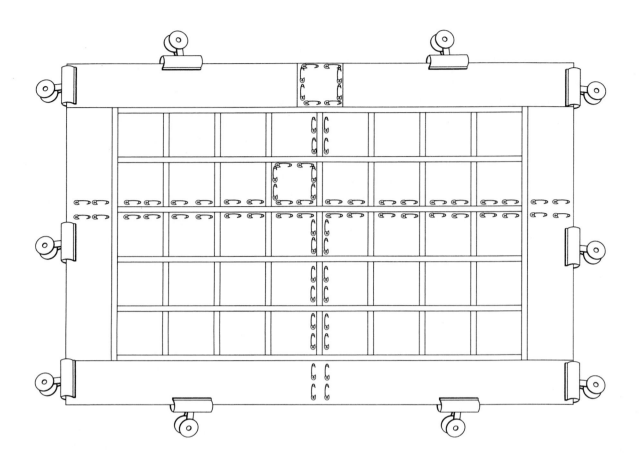

DIAGRAM 12-13

Clamp quilt layers to cutting boards, then pin through the layers, beginning with a "plus" sign through the center rows. Continue pinning each block, working from the center towards the outer edges.

centers of the quilt, placing two pins an inch above and an inch below the lattice strips in each block. Be sure to leave enough room between the pins and the lattice for the sewing machine foot to pass without having to remove the pins (Diagram 12-13).

- Continue pinning from the center out, placing six to eight pins in each block. First, fill the upper left quarter of the quilt, continuing the pins right out into the borders. Next, working from the center, pin the upper right quarter.

- As you pin the lower half of the quilt, you may come to the edge of the cutting boards. Completely pin as far as you can, without going over the edge. Then remove all the clips and carefully slide the three quilt layers along the cutting boards until the unpinned areas are on top. Smooth the backing, batting and quilt top, and clamp to the cutting boards. Continue pinning from the center out, until the whole quilt has been basted.

- Unclamp the quilt and trim any excess batting, leaving about 1" extra all around. Do not trim the backing at this time.

MACHINE QUILTING

Machine quilting in straight lines is very similar to sewing straight seams – just bulkier. If you have pin-basted your quilt according to directions, the three layers can now be treated as a single, thicker layer.

It is helpful to reduce the pressure on your sewing machine foot slightly to allow for smoother feeding of the quilt, with less rippling on the back. Some machines have a round "pop-up" adjustment above the sewing head; others have an adjustment wheel inside the head, next to the light. Some machines adjust automatically.

You can purchase a special "walking foot" attachment that reduces pull on thicker fabrics and results in smoother quilting. On a Bernina sewing machine, the old-style blind hem foot has a metal "plow" running through the center that can be used as a guide for quilting "in the ditch" (in the depression formed where two seams meet).

Use good quality, smoke colored nylon quilting thread in the top part of your machine. Use a regular weight, ordinary sewing thread to match your quilt back in the bobbin. Don't use nylon thread in your bobbin – it alters the tension and creates a mess of loops and snags.

Don't be put off by the nylon thread. If you remember the terrible stuff that knotted and twisted a couple of decades ago, be advised that today's nylon thread is as soft as regular thread and much easier to handle than the old kind.

The dark or "smoke" colored nylon is used for most colored fabrics. The clear nylon is only for white or very light colored fabrics. On anything darker, the clear nylon sparkles in the light and is no longer invisible.

You can buy nylon thread on a plastic bobbin, or in larger amounts on small plastic or cardboard cones. Put the cone in a small empty jar at the back of your sewing machine. Tape a small safety pin, circle end up, to the spool holder on your machine, and run the nylon filament through the circle like an "eye." Continue threading your machine in the normal way, and you will find the nylon thread feeds well without getting tangled, or slipping off the end of the spool.

If you cannot obtain the nylon, or prefer not to use it, try a good quality sewing thread that blends well with the colors of your quilt (gray is a good color). Do not use quilting thread in your sewing machine – it will upset the tension and adjustment.

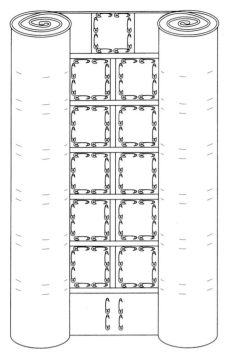

DIAGRAM 12-14
Roll quilt like a scroll to reduce bulk. Roll edges towards center and roll/unroll as you quilt the top.

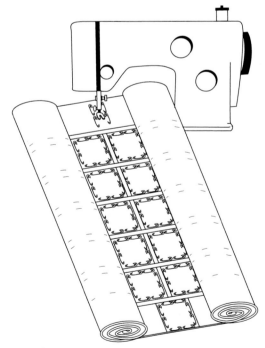

DIAGRAM 12-15
Keep quilt tightly rolled so it will fit under your sewing machine. Support the weight of the quilt with tables behind and beside your machine.

Before you start quilting, make sure your machine has been cleaned and oiled. Use a new needle. Set the stitch for a little longer than you normally use for sewing. Reduce the top tension slightly. Always begin with a full bobbin – it's really frustrating to run out in the middle of a line! It's a good idea to fill a second bobbin in your quilt back color, because it takes more than one to finish the project.

Because the quilt is so large, it will not fit through the sewing machine. To cut down on bulk, keep the quilt rolled in from the edges, like a scroll (Diagram 12-14).

Quilting always begins in the center and moves towards the edges. To reach the center, spread the quilt on a table, right side up, and tightly roll the short edges from the right and from the left, towards the center. As you move across the quilt surface, continue rolling and unrolling the quilt to reach the area you need. If you keep the quilt tightly rolled, it will easily fit under your machine (Diagram 12-15).

It's important to support the weight of the quilt as you sew, otherwise your stitches will be uneven. Set your sewing machine on a small table with another table directly behind it, and one on the left-hand side. I use a card table behind my machine, raised to the level of my machine with bricks and books under the legs. On the left side of the machine, I adjust my ironing board to the correct level. This gives me a large area to support the quilt as it feeds through the machine.

It's a good idea to do some practice quilting before you begin. Layer two large squares of fabric with batting in the middle, draw several lines on the fabric and practice until you feel comfortable. Try rolling the edges, and check to make sure the back of your piece is smooth and pucker-free. Adjust your machine to the correct tension and stitch length.

Begin quilting the Flavor Quilt by stitching a "+" through the center (Diagram 12-16).

- Use a disappearing marking pen and a ruler to extend the 1"-wide lattice strips into the border. Do NOT use the "wash away" type of marking pens or pencils. These require water to remove them, and remember that water will fade the soft drink squares. The disappearing marking pen, usually purple, fades away several hours after an application. In humid weather it may vanish within minutes. Start by marking the vertical and horizontal centers. Do not mark through the dedication block.

- Roll the two short edges of the quilt tightly towards the center, and slide the quilt under the needle until the needle is positioned precisely "in the ditch" where the seams join in the center of the hanging. Position the needle in the fabric by hand, then adjust your stitch length to the shortest possible stitch (the machine will just barely be moving forward). Sew about a quarter of an inch using this miniscule stitch length to lock the thread into the fabric. You will always begin and end this way, rather than backstitching. If you backstitch during machine quilting, your stops and starts will show up as an unsightly lump. Changing to an extremely tiny stitch will invisibly lock the thread permanently in the fabric. The thread ends can be trimmed right to the surface of the fabric, so they don't show.

Whenever you stop sewing in mid-line to change stitch length or rearrange the bulk of the quilt, always leave your needle in the "down" position – in the fabric. If you leave your needle "up," the weight of the quilt will make it slide out of place and your next stitch will be distorted.

- After you have locked the thread in the fabric, leave the needle down and adjust

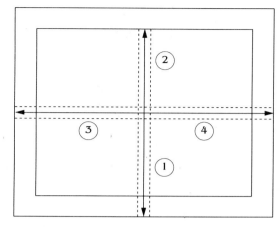

DIAGRAM 12-16
Begin quilting in the center, following the arrows and working in numerical order.

your stitch length to a medium setting (slightly larger than your regular stitch length), and continue to sew, in the ditch, down to the edge of the border. Return to the extra small stitch for the last quarter inch to lock the thread.

- Repeat this same process on the other side of the lattice strip.

- Remove the quilt from the machine, turn it around, and repeat the process, starting in the center (right next to your previous starting stitches). Sew on both sides of the center lattice strip. If you have used a dedication block, do not extend the quilting into the border. You will quilt each side of this block, in the seams, when the rest of the surface has been quilted.

- Remove the quilt from the machine and unroll it on a table. Re-roll the quilt horizontally, rolling the long top and bottom edges towards the center.

- Slide the rolled quilt under the machine until the needle is positioned at the center. You will need to pleat or "bunch" the quilt in your lap, or rest it on your left shoulder as you sew. Lock your stitches, then sew down one side of the center lattice strip. Towards the border, you may find the fabric begins to ripple slightly and bunch up under the presser foot. Use your hands to feed the fabric through smoothly, without distorting the corners of each block. Hold the fabric flat with both hands positioned either side of the needle. It helps to have your right hand a little ahead of the needle to prevent puckers. Lock stitch at the end of the line, return to the center and repeat the process on the other side of the central lattice strip.

- Remove the quilt from the machine, turn it, and repeat the process to sew the two center lines. Remember to begin in the center of the quilt, right next to your pre-

vious stitches.

- Spread the quilt on a table and check your quilting. Make sure there are no pleats or puckers on the back or the front. The quilt is now divided into four quarters. We will finish the machine quilting one quarter at a time.

- Begin quilting the bottom right hand quarter by drawing all the vertical lines into the border. Roll the quilt tightly, short ends towards the center, and stitch on each side of every lattice strip, beginning with the vertical lattice closest to the center of the quilt. Each stitch line begins at the top of the quarter (the previously sewn central horizontal line) and continues to the raw edge of the border. As you complete each pair of lines, move to the next row by rolling up the quilt from the left, and unrolling it from the right. Keep the quilt tightly rolled so your stitching surface is smooth.

- Spread the quilt flat on a table and extend the horizontal lattice lines into the border of the bottom right-hand quarter. Roll the quilt horizontally, long edges towards the center.

- Begin sewing the horizontal line closest to the center. You will stitch from the middle of the quilt out to the border. As you complete each pair of lines, roll the quilt tightly towards the right, and unroll it from the left. Use your hands to keep the surface smooth and to avoid puckers and pleats as you cross your previous stitch lines.

- Spread the quilt flat on a table and mark the vertical lines in the lower left quarter. Roll the quilt very tightly, and stitch as before, beginning with the line closest to the center, and rolling the bulk of the quilt to the right as you go. You will need to keep the quilt very tightly rolled in order for it to move freely under the machine. If the quilt becomes too bulky to move freely, your stitches will be distorted and puckering will occur. If this happens, it's a good idea to stop sewing, spread the quilt out on a table and roll it tightly again.

- When all the vertical lines in the quarter are sewn, mark and sew the horizontal lines. Again, be careful when you cross your vertical stitch lines. You may have to manipulate your fabric by pulling or pushing, to feed it smoothly under the needle. It may even be necessary to move some of the basting pins to avoid creating a pleat.

- When the bottom two quarters of the quilt have been sewn, turn the quilt around and finish the top two quarters the same way, beginning with the upper left quarter (which is now the lower right quarter). When all vertical and horizontal lines have been sewn, stitch on each side of the dedication block.

- You have now finished quilting your wall hanging. If you used invisible thread your quilting will only show in the borders. Remove all the basting pins except those in the four corners. Turn the quilt over to admire your work. You are now ready for the final job, the binding.

BINDING AND FINISHING THE QUILT

Finishing the Flavor Quilt requires just a few more steps: trimming the edges; making a sleeve; sewing the binding; and signing your artwork.

TRIMMING THE EDGES
- Spread the quilt on a table with a cutting mat underneath a corner. Remove the corner pin. Accurately position the right angle corner of your largest quilting ruler exactly at the corner of the quilt. You may need to rearrange the quilt slightly to conform.
- Use a rotary cutter to trim the corner

exactly. You should be trimming off batting and backing, but not the quilt top. Try not to cut into the extra backing fabric, as this will be used to make a sleeve. Replace the pin to hold the three layers together in the corner.

- Repeat this process until all four corners have been accurately trimmed.
- Use the straight edge of the large ruler to trim the areas between the corners.

MAKING A SLEEVE
The easiest way to hang a quilt is to use a built-in "sleeve." This is a tube of fabric, sewn to the back of the quilt along the top edge. Since this sleeve will carry the full weight of the quilt, it should be sturdily stitched by machine, rather than tacked on by hand.

- Retrieve the remaining backing fabric cut from the bottom edge of the quilt. It should extend the full width of the quilt, and will be about 10-12" wide, depending upon whether you used a sheet or fabric for the backing.
- Using the ripped or sheet edge as your guide, fold this strip in half, and then in half again, matching the edges for strip cutting. Press. Trim the uneven edges of each side of the folded strip through all four layers to get a single long strip, all the same width, at least 8" wide and the length of the quilt (about 82").
- Measure about 3" in from the ends of the strip, fold to the wrong side and press. Fold the entire strip in half lengthwise, wrong sides together, being sure that the raw edges are even. Press. Find the center of your sleeve by folding it in half. Mark the center with a pin.
- Find the center of the quilt's top edge by folding it in half and marking with a pin (it will be in the middle of the dedication block). Match the center of the sleeve to the center of the quilt and pin it to the

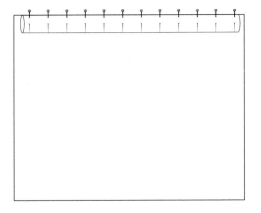

DIAGRAM 12-17
Pin sleeve to back of quilt.

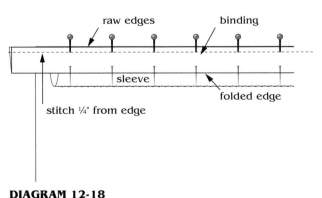

raw edges

binding

sleeve

folded edge

stitch ¼" from edge

DIAGRAM 12-18
Sew binding with ¼" seam through quilt and sleeve.

back, carefully keeping all the raw edges even. Pin the sleeve from the center out towards the edges. You will need to stretch the quilt slightly as you pin, otherwise there will be pleats under the sleeve. The two ends of the sleeve should be at least two to three inches from the side edges of the quilt (Diagram 12-17).

BINDING THE QUILT

Bed quilts require bias binding that "gives" slightly as the quilt is tossed around during use. Wallhangings, however, can be bound with straight grain fabric, since there will be little wear and tear. This is the simplest type of binding. Since it stretches very little, straight grain binding requires squared-off corners, rather than mitered or rounded edges. A separate piece of binding is used for each of the four edges.

• Retrieve the binding strip made earlier in the project. It is a 2" wide strip, joined into a single long piece with seams pressed open. The long strip is folded in half along its length and pressed to form a double piece, 1" wide.

• Working from the back, or wrong side of the quilt, begin binding the top edge. Allow the binding to extend about 1" beyond the quilt corner. Be sure all raw edges are even as you sew. Use a quarter-inch seam allowance, and sew carefully to make sure the seam is straight and accurate (Diagram 12-18).

• When you come to the beginning of the sleeve, backstitch for about an inch to secure the sleeve end. Be sure to keep gentle pressure on the quilt as you sew, pulling it towards you, away from the needle, to make sure the quilt is fully extended. If you do not stretch it, the quilt will bunch up and create pleats and puckers. Double stitch the sleeve end.

- Cut the excess binding, leaving a 1" extension beyond the quilt edge.

- Pin the sleeve flat against the back of the quilt. Sew the bottom edge of the sleeve to the quilt back, using your machine's blind hem stitch. To do so, fold the quilt so the sleeve edge extends about ¼", just as if it were the hem of a skirt. Be sure your "blind" stitches only catch the quilt back. They should not show on the front of the quilt. If you are unable to do a blind hem stitch on your machine, sew the bottom of the sleeve to the back by hand, using a long whipstitch. Remove all pins.

- Working on the right side of the quilt, pull the folded edge of the binding over the raw edges until it meets the line of stitching on the front. Pin in place so the stitch line does not show. Position your needle so it is very close to the folded edge of the binding where it meets the quilt top and top stitch through all layers. Trim the ends of the binding even with the quilt sides (Diagram 12-19).

- Repeat the binding process along the bottom of the quilt, being careful to stretch the quilt to its full width as you sew. Remember to apply the binding to the back of the quilt, then flip it to the front and top stitch.

- To bind the sides of the quilt, start sewing from the back, leaving ½" of binding extending beyond the top and bottom quilt edges. Before pinning the binding to the front, fold these ½" extensions to the inside of the binding and pin. Next, fold the binding to the front, adjusting the corner folds as necessary to make a neat finish. Top stitch through all the layers backstitching at the beginning and end (Diagram 12-20).

Signing Your Quilt

Any work of art is more valuable if it is

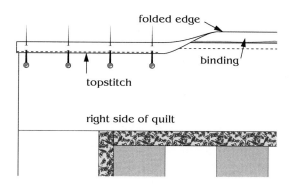

DIAGRAM 12-19
Fold binding to stitch line on front of quilt. Pin; top stitch close to folded edge. Trim ends of binding even with quilt sides.

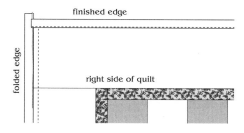

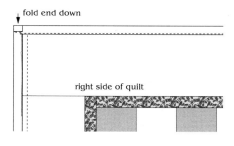

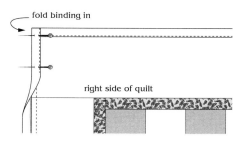

DIAGRAM 12-20

signed and dated. Since this is such an unusual quilt, it's a good idea to add all the information you can, so future generations will understand what you did.

Use an extra fine point permanent marking pen to write important facts on the back of the quilt. Give the name of the quilt, who made it, where and when. Provide cleaning information and warn against washing with detergent, if you have dyed with soft drink mix, and storing in high heat (such as a car's trunk in summer) that could fade the crayons. Be sure to photograph your quilt for a permanent record.

Hanging Your Quilt

Hang your quilt where it will be safe from touching hands. A library is a good place, because it's usually clean and air-conditioned. Book shelves also create a visual and physical barrier, discouraging people from getting too close, or touching the quilt.

A wooden, plastic or metal rod can be used for hanging, or the quilt can be suspended on vinyl-covered clothes line. Whatever you use, it should be rigid, so the quilt does not sag or bunch. New wood should be painted so it doesn't damage or stain the fabric. The sleeve will pro-tect the quilt back.

Be careful not to display your quilt in strong natural or artificial light. Both sunshine and fluorescent lights will change the crayon colors, and eventually make them fade. Intense heat will also cause the crayon colors to fade.

Many people assume the best way to protect a quilt is to spray it with stain-repelling chemicals, or to hang it under glass.

I worry that spraying the quilt will cause a chemical reaction, over time, with the colors used. I do not recommend it. Textiles should not be sealed behind glass, because moisture – especially in hot, humid climates – will cause mildew, and will eventually destroy the fabric. Heat also builds up behind the glass, causing the crayons to fade.

Some of my school quilts have been successfully placed behind a free-hanging sheet of Plexiglass. The plastic barrier allows air circulation on the sides, but prevents easy access to the quilt, thus keeping it clean and protected in high-traffic areas. This is a fairly expensive method, however, and light reflection often makes the quilt hard to see.

Treat your masterpiece carefully, and it should last for many, many years.

The School Quilt Project

The Flavor Quilt Project can be conducted on many different levels. It can be as simple as working with your own children, or a group of friends. It can be offered as a Scout project, or a Bible School creation. It can be a half-day workshop at a store or a museum, or a one-day workshop, involving adults, children, or both. It can also be a week-long, or even months-long program, in school or after school. The beauty of this project is its flexibility. Take these techniques, add children and presto! You have instant fun!

The Flavor Quilt has been extremely successful as a school project, but if you are not a classroom teacher, working in a school setting can be intimidating. When administrators start tossing around terms like "lesson plans," "integration into the curriculum" and "keeping children on task," the average non-teacher can quickly feel out of her depth.

One of the first decisions to make is whether or not you are working for money. If you are offering the project on a volunteer basis, you should be able to call the shots. If the school is paying you to run the project, you may have to follow more stringent guidelines.

FUNDING

Money for art projects is available from many different sources, including private donations all the way up to official support from government agencies.

The first place to look for funding is within your community: from your local arts organization, museum or library. Your school parent-teacher organization may offer financial support, or businesses in the community may sponsor the project. If these avenues are not productive, try your state arts organization.

Those who are interested in working in schools on a regular basis should investigate the Arts in Education program in their state.

Arts in Education (AIE) is a nationwide program sponsored by the National Endowment for the Arts and administered in each state by an arts commission or similar government agency. The program places professional artists who are on an approved artist roster in residence in schools and community organizations for one to 32 weeks. AIE is a unique interaction with visual, literary, media and performing artists, designed to awaken and reinforce the natural creativity of participants, build arts audiences for the future, and bring the artistic process into peoples' lives.

There may be several ways for artists in your state to qualify for the program, but usually samples of work must be submitted to a review board. In most cases, the review board for a particular discipline convenes annually, so it may take up to a year to apply. Once approved, artists may offer themselves to schools and community organizations that receive matching funds in the program.

Some state AIE programs are more organized than others. In some states, approved artists have to negotiate all their own residencies, fees, contracts etc. Other states have an annual or twice-yearly booking conference which brings together the approved artists and representatives of schools and organizations.

Fees paid to artists vary widely. They

may be standardized, or the artists may be allowed to negotiate their own rates. The fees may be in two segments: one for professional services, and a separate fee for materials. Some states include a small sum to cover expenses for travel, lodging and food; others do not. The artist is usually considered to be a self-employed independent contractor. This means that no taxes are withheld from fees, and the artist is responsible for these payments to the IRS.

The AIE program has very specific guidelines for residencies, including the number, type and length of classes and the number of students involved. Artists are required to submit pre- and post-residency suggestions, lesson plans, samples of students' work, or slides of the project, in addition to evaluations.

Some sponsors pay the artist at the end of the residency, while others delay payment for weeks while official invoices work their way up the bureaucratic ladder, sometimes all the way to the state treasurer's office! When you're dealing with government, it can take forever to get paid at the end of a fiscal year or while the legislature's not in session!

In addition to the AIE program, schools can apply for other types of financial help for special projects: grants, mini grants, incentive grants, target grants, matching funds and what-have-you. Unless you are an experienced grant-writer, have somebody at the school apply. The paperwork involved is phenomenal. One funding category in my files requires that an original and 21 collated copies be submitted for consideration! If your grant application involves 27 pages, plus additional support material, you'd go broke just paying for all those copies to be made!

Remember, too, that the wheels of government grind slowly. You may have to apply for funding a whole school year in advance of your project, and wait for months before you find out whether your grant has been approved.

Apart from official government agencies, funding can also be secured from other sources. The school's PTA or PTO may be interested in supporting the project. A related business, service club or religious group in the community may provide funds. A school fund-raiser (garage sale, spaghetti supper) could support the project. If there is an active quilt guild in the community, this would make a perfect outreach project. A number of national quilt organizations and local arts organizations also offer personal grants for artists to conduct deserving projects.

If funding for a salary is not possible, at least check with local businesses to provide the necessary materials either free, or at cost.

CURRICULUM-BASED THEMES

Once you have "sold" the school on your residency (either literally or figuratively), the next step is to decide what type of quilt you will make. Students love the miniature quilts because they keep the final product. Principals love the large group quilts that can hang in the school office or library.

One way to "sell" the quilt to school administrators is to show how the project can be incorporated into the curriculum. Pulling students out of class for a week to create a quilt may seem too frivolous to many administrators. Integrate that same quilt into the curriculum and you have a whole new approach! Now the quilt becomes an "enrichment" tool rather than a waste of time.

Several years ago, Nancy Taylor Smith and Debbie Reid, two elementary teachers in Charlotte, North Carolina, wrote an entire semester's curriculum around quilting. They called their project "The Patchwork Quilt Curriculum."

The semester began with the reading of "Sarah, Plain and Tall" by the third grade and "The Wright Brothers at Kitty Hawk" for the fourth graders. It expanded through the showing of family quilts, "reading" quilts as a form of folklore and storytelling, learning patterns of quiltmaking from diverse cultures, developing skills in quilt pattern and color design, freehand drawing, dyeing and sewing of patches, letter writing and descriptive essay writing, and culminating in the actual construction of a large Flavor Quilt.

The third and fourth grade teachers who joined "The Patchwork Quilt Curriculum" used the two novels as the foundation for their language arts lessons, then expanded this common topic into a multi-disciplinary curriculum encompassing not only language arts, but also history, art, social studies and geometry.

The project blossomed to draw in parents, grandparents, neighbors and others connected with the school who shared old family quilts, oral histories and memories of both the school and the community, and of life as it used to be.

By the time I arrived to create the Flavor Quilt just before Christmas, the students in the project knew almost as much about quilting as I did! They had discovered a deep appreciation for both quilts and women's place in history through their classroom studies and the many field trips and enrichment opportunities created by the unique curriculum.

"The Newell Quilt," named for their school, included designs representing Colonial life, historic landmarks and state symbols. It was an extremely colorful quilt, with many exceptional designs. The crowning glory for the entire project was the blue ribbon the quilt won at the Charlotte Quilters' Guild show the following year.

SETTING UP A RESIDENCY

Once funding has been secured, make sure you have a legal contract, spelling out such things as dates, location and fees.

Meet with the sponsors to find out about their particular needs and goals, and to choose a suitable space for classes. You'll need a room large enough for up to 30 people, a sink and water, good light, at least six large tables, chairs for everyone, and a floor that can be either cleaned or covered. You will also need a pencil sharpener, electrical outlets, garbage cans, paper towels and soap.

Ideally, you should have the same room for the entire residency. Moving from room to room requires too much time between classes. Hopefully, you will be the only person using the room, so you can leave equipment set up, and fabric drying without being disturbed.

Although this preparation can be done by letter or telephone, there's no substitute for actually visiting the site and talking directly with the organizers.

Ask the sponsors to select a theme for a large quilt. Be sure the theme is realistic for the age group. I've had some pretty sophisticated themes suggested that would have been very difficult for the proposed grade level to carry through successfully.

Be sure the sponsors allow enough time for children to explore the theme thoroughly before the residency. During a one-week session, there is no time for research. Each child must already know what he or she is to draw.

Penny Summers, highly organized coordinator of media services for Calhoun County Public Schools in St. Matthews, South Carolina, used index cards to help her middle school students prepare for quilt projects.

Each student chose a book related to the quilts' themes (one was state history, the other international folklore) from the library, read the book, then summarized the information on a 5" x 8" index card. On the back of his/her card, each student drew a picture to illustrate the book. Each card was identified with the name of the student and the classroom teacher. The cards were handed out at the beginning of each art session, and the students immediately knew what to draw, and how to adapt the designs as necessary, based on the information on the cards.

At the end of the two projects, students created a book for each quilt which included all the research information and a key identifying each block, its maker and its significance.

When you discuss a school quilt, suggest ways to integrate the project into the curriculum: a social studies project could be a state quilt, or a history quilt; a language arts project could be a library quilt, a folklore quilt, or a quilt illustrating a particular book; an oral history quilt could feature illustrations, and be accompanied by tape recorded stories for each picture; a science project could be a fossil or dinosaur quilt or a space quilt; a math project could be geometric designs; even a physical education project could illustrate sports! You could also try general topics, such as a school quilt, a family life quilt, a "favorite things" quilt, a seasons quilt, a special program quilt, an art/music/drama quilt, a guidance quilt, a retirement or fund-raising quilt, or a school anniversary quilt. The list is quite endless. The quilt is only the medium: the message can be anything!

Be sure to suggest that students practice sewing before the project. If each child can thread a needle, tie a knot and make a simple stitch, you won't need as much volunteer help for the sewing segments.

Provide the sponsors with written information about the project, including brief lesson plans, class size, number and length of classes, a suggested schedule, and a list of things you'll need.

Be sure to discuss volunteers. If parents are unavailable, ask for friends or relatives. Contact a senior citizens' group or retirement home, a local quilt/embroidery/smocking group or service club. Request help from unassigned school staff – I've recruited principals, office workers, cafeteria personnel, custodians and bus drivers! If all else fails, use students in the older grades to help with the younger kids. Be sure your young helpers know how to sew and have a responsible attitude.

It's a good idea to have a brief meeting with these volunteers before class and show them exactly what you want them to do. The best situation is to have the same volunteers for a full day, or even for a full week. It saves having to teach new helpers for every class.

SCHEDULING

Most of us don't realize how much work goes into setting up a school schedule. Teachers are required to cover a certain amount of material in a certain amount of time, and when you start pulling kids out of class for other projects, you often run into trouble.

One reason younger children are chosen for this project is that their schedules are more flexible. Once you get into the older grades, arranging for the same students to be in the same place at the same time every day for a week can be impossible! This is another selling point for a curriculum-based theme: call it a social studies project, and the quilt can be made during social studies classes each day.

A successful week-long residency is based on 100 students, who meet with the artist each day for 45 minutes. At least 15 minutes between classes is required to prepare materials. If one class arrives as the previous class leaves, you'll never have the sewing sorted out, or the needles threaded.

A sample schedule for the week might include the following: Monday, 8:45 to 9:30 a.m. (assembly for all four classes to introduce the project); then individual classes in the art area, 10:15 to 11; 11:15 to 12; 12:30 to 1:15; 1:30 to 2:15. Tuesday through Thursday, classes run from 9 to 9:45; 10 to 10:45; 11 to 11:45; 12:30 to 1:15. Friday is a studio day for the artist to finish the quilt without the students.

Other scheduling options might include doing the introduction for each of the four classes individually on Monday, and using Friday for additional classes, leaving the final construction for the weekend, or following week. Classes could also be conducted one day a week for five weeks, if time allows.

Make sure the classroom teachers understand that they will be participating in the project. You will need the help of someone who can keep discipline while you work. Students are also more motivated when they see their teacher is interested in the project.

LESSON PLANS

A lesson plan is nothing more than a list of things you plan to do each day, a "road map" for each class.

When you plan your project, decide what you will do each day, what materials you will need to accomplish this goal, and how much time each class will require.

Remember to tailor your plan to the age group. Older children will need a more sophisticated project and a different time span to accomplish the goal. Since older students often create more detailed art, they may actually need more time for the art sessions than younger children. On the other hand, older children usually sew a lot faster than younger ones, and they'll finish the sewing portion of the project more quickly than a younger group.

It may help to write the entire project down on paper. Make a list of topics to be covered in each class, materials and classroom equipment needed, and time required. Use this list to make sure you have all materials with you each day. Be aware of how much time it takes to complete each process, and pace yourself and your student's work accordingly.

Don't forget specialized vocabulary. Make sure the students understand the terms you're using. For younger grades, a word chart is often helpful. You may need to repeat definitions and explanations each day.

Here is a sample outline for the large Flavor Quilt. All classes last 45 minutes.

CLASS #1
Assembly to introduce the project

Divide the presentation into three 15-minute segments.

First segment

Ask if students have quilts of their own; invite them to bring their quilts to school. Talk about the quilt as a "fiber sandwich," demonstrating the layers in a hoop and discussing the construction of a quilt. Talk about cotton and how it is grown and turned into fabric. Give a brief history of quilting and its importance as women's art. Use question and answer format.

Second segment

Show a 15-minute video or slide show (geared to the age group) about cotton or quilting.

Third segment

Using many different examples (your own quilts, or borrowed ones), show how a quilt is constructed of blocks, naming the different patterns of the examples. Be sure to include pieces of your own work, and end with an example of a full-sized Flavor Quilt, similar to the one they'll be making.

CLASS #2
First art period

Hang a completed Flavor Quilt in the classroom for a reference. Decorate the walls with quilts or quilt pictures. Arrange the classroom with five tables, each with a basket of fabric crayons. Conduct the class from a table placed in front of the sink.

During this class, each student will create a small drawing and color it with fabric crayons for use in the Nine-Patch blocks. Each student will also dye a fabric square in soft drink dye, and make an autographed handprint on the quilt border.

At the beginning of the class, discuss each of the three tasks in detail. Explain how to use the crayons (be sure to mention reverse images and the fact that pencil lines don't transfer to the cloth). Show finished examples.

Mix the soft drink dye and have the teacher supervise this process while you do the handprints. Depending on the age group, you may need volunteers to supervise hand-washing and the drawing activity. Take two students at a time for handprints and dyeing, while the rest work on their pictures. Keep close watch on the clock to make sure all activities are finished in 45 minutes.

For student homework: each table must work as a team to produce an idea for a large crayon design for the following day. It's a good idea for students to bring 7¾" sketches to the next day's class. You should have five teams/drawings from each of the four classes.

Your homework: meet with the project coordinator to assign the dedication block; give 7¾" paper square and a pack of fabric crayons to the artist (student or teacher) chosen; transfer all the small crayon designs to cloth and outline each one.

CLASS #3
Second art period

Before your first class arrives, remove the dyed fabric from the dye buckets and set it out to dry. Rinse and dry the fabric again during your lunch break.

Keeping the same room set-up, divide the class into five groups to make the large crayon squares. Clear part of your table for an ironing area.

Before you begin, review ways to use the crayons, reverse images, pencil lines, etc. Teach reverse image lettering to older children, using a sunny window as a light box.

Make sure the team members cooperate, with everybody helping to color the team square. In a 45-minute class, there is not time to work individually on the large square. Team members will all have to color at the same time by placing the square in the center of the table. It's a good idea to have a color conference first, so nobody colors an area purple that's supposed to be green! The classroom teacher can be a mediator/cheerleader during this session, allowing you some time to work on the small designs, or to complete unfinished handprints.

As soon as a group has finished, have that team watch you transferring the design to cloth. While you're ironing, explain the transfer process, what materials they'll need and where they can buy fabric crayons. Show the finished transfer to the whole class.

During any remaining class time, allow students to create their own designs to take home and iron onto cloth or a shirt.

Student homework: practice sewing small stitches on a straight line.

Your homework: steam press all the dyed squares; finish transferring and outlining all the designs; pin all the squares together ready for sewing; thread needles.

CLASS #4
First day of sewing

Keep the same room set-up, but exchange the crayon baskets for sewing baskets, complete with all necessary equipment. Meet with your volunteers before class to explain what you want them to do. Place a teacher or volunteer at each table.

Follow the suggested introduction detailed in the Teaching Children to Sew chapter. Use finished examples to illustrate your talk. Although this introduction may seem to take up too much time, I have found that children of all ages sew much better with it than without it, so don't be tempted to skip this step!

Stand over each child and demonstrate the first three stitches, then let the table volunteer take over any problems that arise. Make sure children check their work before turning it in.

Your job will be to examine each piece as it's returned, iron it and pin the next piece to it. Don't let the children get ahead of you! You'll have to work fast to keep them supplied with new sewing, especially when they get the hang of it!

Be sure to end the class right on time, or you won't be ready for the next group. Unfinished pieces should be left for the next class to work on. Have the volunteers thread needles while you check, iron and pin.

Student homework: look for quilts or quilt-related items to bring to school.

Your homework: iron and trim all the finished Nine-Patch blocks to size; arrange the quilt in rows, decide on final placement and

code each block; pin everything to be sewn; thread needles.

CLASS #5
Second sewing period

Keep the same room set-up, with a volunteer at each table. Ask for show and tell of quilts, or shirts with students' designs. Display new examples of your current work. Explain how you will finish the quilt, showing the dedication block. Talk about where the finished quilt will hang and how the students can take care of it. Review the sewing procedure.

Continue sewing the quilt until all five rows are complete, eight blocks in each row. Clear table or floor space and set the quilt pieces together, the way they will be joined. Invite everyone to view the almost-finished quilt. Take plenty of photographs!

If time allows, students may make more designs to keep, using fabric crayons. You may also provide quilt books or magazines for browsing, or photocopied quilt designs for coloring. Students could write essays, letters or poems about the project. They could learn how to draft quilting designs such as Feather Wreath, using a plate and spoon, or Clamshell, using a teacup.

Student homework: learn how to take good care of family quilts and obtain a written or oral history for each one. Continue quilt research in libraries, in museums or at quilt shows.

Your homework: complete the quilt, photograph it and return it to the school.

HELPFUL HINTS

Don't panic, be flexible and keep your sense of humor!

Working in a different school almost every week, I have learned to adapt quickly to changing situations. One freezing Monday morning I arrived at a rural school in the middle of a cow pasture to find there was no water in the art portable. A custodian used a blowtorch to thaw the plastic pipes before the first class arrived. We had cold water – very cold water!

Another Monday, somebody let off a stink bomb in the high school. Smelly. Very smelly. On still another Monday, a principal decided she'd rather have a full-sized quilt than the miniature quilts I'd spent days cutting out and packaging. Another time I checked every restroom in the school for paper towels and found only blow dryers. We sent a custodian to the nearest grocery store.

SPACE PROBLEMS

It's important to set limits and know what you can and cannot do. More than once, in overcrowded schools, I've been asked to conduct my project on a stage with poor light, no water, and a noisy cafeteria on the other side of the curtains. On one stage I was expected to work on the floor, because there weren't enough tables and chairs! I had to refuse, because I knew the project could not work under such conditions. If you push hard enough, a classroom or similar space can usually be found.

I once worked quite successfully in a hallway, with buckets of water on chairs for handwashing. It was a wide and well-lit hall, and it worked well, except when the entire kindergarten contingent marched through twice a day at lunch.

OVERCROWDING

Another difficult situation to handle is the school that "can't leave anyone out." They want you to work with a much larger group, or with extra classes, either because "the kids' feelings will be hurt" or because "the parents just won't understand why little Johnny couldn't participate."

If you think you can handle this type of request, you could redesign the project to make a larger quilt; make more than one quilt; or require additional payment for your extra work.

If you don't want to change your project, you will have to insist on limits. Having too many children in a project makes it very hard on both you and the kids. The 100-student limit assures every child a quality experience.

If there are more than four classes in a grade level, the teachers can decide who would like to participate, or they can draw straws. In a school that has multiple art residencies each year, teachers are often given their choice of one project.

VOLUNTEERS

One of the most common problems you'll face is the case of the vanishing volunteers. People promise to come and then don't show up, or somebody forgets to find help. It's time for an "all points bulletin" to the office to round up anyone in the building who can help. If there are no adults, send to the oldest grade for students – they'll volunteer in a hurry!

BE PREPARED

The two comments I hear most often are: "You're so organized" and "You're so patient." My family would find both these statements hilarious, because my home is a complete disaster and I'm always yelling about something.

In the classroom, however, organization is everything. This project cannot run smoothly unless you are totally prepared, and do a lot of after-hours work.

"Keeping your cool" is also vitally important. You'll soon notice that the very best teachers never need to yell. Lowering your voice is often effective in grabbing kids' attention. Yell at them all day and they'll ignore you. Besides, you'll develop a terribly sore throat.

DISCIPLINE

In every group of children, there's always one who'll drive you crazy. Watch the child's teacher for clues. It helps to have a quiet word with the teacher to identify children with genuine problems. Some of these problems can be heartbreaking or hair-raising, and it's well worth your time to get the facts before you act.

A child who doesn't follow directions may have special needs, may be on medication or may have a disability. Often such children respond well to a little extra attention, and with help, can have a truly successful experience. For many such children, success at school is quite rare. It's a good feeling to know you have helped to build a child's fragile self-esteem.

On the other hand, there will always be children who simply behave badly. Expect the classroom teacher to maintain discipline, since you have little official authority. Real behavior problems should be removed. If a class is truly "out of control," I will stop teaching until the kids behave. Thankfully, this doesn't happen often, because most children really enjoy the project.

SETTING UP A HALF-DAY OR
ONE-DAY WORKSHOP

The Flavor Quilt Project can be used as a half-day or full-day workshop, but it requires plenty of advance preparation. Use the information in this book as a guide, and refer to the "Making a Miniature" chapter for specific directions.

The project should be designed for adult/child teams. Each child should be accompanied by an adult, or responsible teenager to work on a miniature quilt.

Be sure participants wear old clothes and plastic aprons. Pre-package the miniature quilt kits in recloseable plastic bags. Each kit should contain all the fabric pieces, already washed, cut and marked with seam lines, batting and paper in the correct sizes. Since the soft drink dyes take more than a day to process, either eliminate the dyeing segment, or include dyed fabric squares in each kit.

Set up the workshop room with plastic-covered tables for paints and stamps, regular tables for crayons and dye sticks. Provide plenty of soap and paper towels. Have trays of paint set out, along with a variety of gadgets for printing, and buckets of water to clean equipment.

You will need several ironing areas. Remind children that these "hot zones" are off limits. Only adults are allowed to iron.

Begin the workshop by explaining the project, showing examples. Take one table at a time and thoroughly explain how each process works. It sounds like a monumental task, but don't forget the adults are there to do the listening, and they will help their children.

During the workshop, your job will be to demonstrate the various techniques, to transfer and heat-set designs, and to suggest ways to decorate the fabric.

When all the squares have been decorated, clear the cleanest tables and set them up with sewing equipment. Discuss quilt construction and demonstrate the running stitch. Encourage the adults to let their children do the work. Too often, adults assume the kids can't sew.

In a half-day workshop, only a few quilts will be completed. Make sure the adults understand how to finish the quilts at home. In a full-day workshop, all the quilts should be completed by the end of the class.

Quilt Books For Children

If you are lucky enough to own family quilts, your children will already know how pretty they are to look at, how nice they are to snuggle under.

Share with them your quilt histories – who made your quilts, why they were made, when they were made, and what they were made of. Share any memories you have of quiltmaking in your family. Ask older family members to share their memories, too.

If your children have family quilts on their beds, encourage them to treat those quilts with respect. Show them a new way of looking at their quilts – not just as covers that keep them warm, but as true works of art, mathematical puzzles involving hours and hours of labor. Let them start seeing quilts as beautiful coverings for walls, as well as beds. Teach them to treasure their quilts as family heirlooms. When your children are adults, they'll be glad their family quilts have been so well looked after.

While you're making group quilts with children, invite people in the community to share their quilts and quilt stories with your young quilters.

Check area museums for quilt collections, take your group to quilt shows or quilt shops. Check your library for books about quilts or quiltmaking.

Here are some good books for children that either deal with the subject of quilts, or have quilts as a significant part of the story.

The Patchwork Farmer, by Craig Brown, Greenwillow Books, 1989. (A delightful picture book without words about a farmer's ripped and patched overalls. Ages 2-6)

Ernest & Celestine's Patchwork Quilt, by Gabrielle Vincent, Greenwillow Books, 1982. (A bear and a mouse make each other a patchwork quilt in this story without words. Ages 2-6)

The Berenstain Bears and Mama's New Job, by Stan & Jan Berenstain, Random House, 1984. (When Mama Bear opens a quilt shop, everyone in the family has to help at home. Ages 3-9)

Bizzy Bones & The Lost Quilt, by Jacqueline Briggs Martin, Lothrop: Lee & Shepard Books, 1988. (When Bizzy Bones loses his special quilt, friends help to make a new one. Ages 3-9)

The Quilt, by Ann Jonas, Greenwillow Books, 1984 (A child's new quilt provides memories and bedtime adventures. Ages 3-6)

Nattie Parsons' Good Luck Lamb, by Lisa Campbell Ernst, Viking Penguin, 1988. (Nattie's lamb has pink wool after a trip to the raspberry patch! Ages 3-10)

On Market Street, by Arnold Lobel, Scholastic Books. (This Caldecott Honor Book is an unusual alphabet, with the Queen dressed in an array of quilts. Ages 3-9)

The Josefina Story Quilt, by Eleanor Coerr, Harper & Row, 1986. (While traveling west with her family in 1850, a young girl makes a patchwork quilt which chronicles her experiences. Ages 4-9)

The Keeping Quilt, by Patricia Polacco, Simon & Schuster, 1988. (A special memory quilt made from the clothing of relatives ties together the lives of four generations of an immigrant family. Ages 4-8)

Sam Johnson and The Blue Ribbon Quilt,

by Lisa Campbell Ernst, Lothrup, 1983. (When his wife's quilting group won't let him join, Sam gathers his men friends to make an award-winning quilt. Wonderful illustrations, with page borders of story-related quilt blocks identified at the end of the book. Ages 3-10)

Picture Pie, A Circle Drawing Book, by Ed Emberly, Little Brown & Co., 1984. (Shows how to cut circles and curves into wonderful shapes that could be made into paper quilts. Ages 5-11)

The Patchwork Quilt, by Valerie Flournoy, Dial Books, 1985. (Using scraps of family clothing, a girl helps her grandmother make a wonderful memory quilt. A Reading Rainbow book, also available on videotape. Ages 6-11)

No Dragons On My Quilt, by Jean Ray Laury, American Quilter's Society, 1990. (When Benjamin is afraid to go to bed by himself, he is comforted by the special quilt his grandmother makes for him. Includes instructions and patterns for making the quilt featured in the story. Ages 3-12)

Patchwork Tales, by Susan L. Roth and Ruth Phang, Atheneum, 1984. (A grandmother tells the family stories about the blocks in a quilt. Illustrated with wood-block prints of the quilt patterns. Ages 6-10)

The Quilt Story, by Tony Johnston, illustrated by Tomie dePaola, G. P. Putnam's Sons, 1985. (A pioneer mother stitches a beautiful quilt for her daughter. Years later, another mother mends and patches it for her little girl. Ages 6-11)

The Mountains of Quilt, by Nancy Willard, illustrated by Tomie dePaola, Dover Publications, 1987. (Magicians turn grandmother's quilt into a magic carpet. Ages 6-10)

The Bedspread, by Sylvia Fair, Wm. Morrow, 1982. (Two elderly sisters embroider their childhood home, with surprising results. Ages 6-11)

Happy Birthday, Kirsten! A Springtime Story, by Jeanne Thieme, Pleasant Co. (Girls make a friendship quilt for their teacher. A tradition of giving friendship quilts in early pioneer history. Ages 7-11)

Jamie and the Mystery Quilt, by V. Erwin, Scholastic, 1987. (Jamie and his friends have adventures looking for the maker of an old quilt. Ages 7-12)

Calico Bush, by Rachel Field, illustrated by Allen Lewis, Dell, first published in 1931. (The classic story of an orphaned pioneer girl offers a historically significant portrait of life in eighteenth century America. Ages 9-adolescent)

Nell's Quilt, by Susan Terris, Farra, 1987. (In 1899, Nell is to be married against her will. As she makes a crazy quilt, she withdraws into a solitary world. Ages: Adolescent)

Sources & Resources

Untreated Muslin for Dyeing with Powdered Soft Drink Mix

M'Art Designs
Marit Lee Kucera
30 South St. Albans, #5
St. Paul, MN 55105
(612) 222-2483
(Five yard minimum order; discounts for 25 yards and over)

——

Fabric Paints and Dyes

Pro Chemical & Dye, Inc.
P. O. Box 14
Somerset, MA 02726
(617) 676-3838

Cerulean Blue, Ltd.
P. O. Box 21168
Seattle, WA 98111-3168
(206) 443-7744

——

Paints, Fabric Crayons, Dye Sticks, School Scissors, Bulldog Clips, and Much More
(All of these companies have annual catalogs filled with tons of art supplies)

Nasco
901 Janesville Ave.
Fort Atkinson, WI 53538
(800) 558-9595

Pyramid Art Supply
Box 877
Urbana, IL 61801-0877
(800) 637-0955

Sax Arts & Crafts
P. O. Box 51710
New Berlin, WI 53151
(800) 558-6696

——

Quilting Supplies

Omnigrid, Inc.
3227-B 164th St. SW
Lynnwood, WA 98037-3237
(800) 543-4206
(Rulers and templates)

Nancy's Notions
P. O. Box 683
Beaver Dam, WI 53916
(414) 887-0690
(Notions, books, catalog)

Harriet's Treadle Arts
7770 W. 44th Ave.
Wheat Ridge, CO 80033
(303) 424-4242 or 424-1290
(Special feet for machine quilting, notions, books, 108" wide muslin, catalog)

Clotilde
1909 S. W. First Ave.
Ft. Lauderdale, FL 33315
(305) 761-8655
(Notions, books, catalog)

Keepsake Quilting
Dover St., P. O. Box 1459
Meredith, NH 03253
(603) 279-3351
(Supplies, books, catalog)

Quilting Books

American Quilter's Society
P. O. Box 3290
Paducah, KY 42002-3290
(800) 626-5420
(Books, discount prices for AQS members)

Quilting Books Unlimited
1911 W. Wilson
Batavia, IL 60510
(800) 347-3261
(Write for catalog of hundreds of quilting books and videos for adults and children; also patterns, notions etc.)

————

Quilt Batting

Hobbs Bonded Fibers
1200 S. McKinney
Mexia, TX 76667
(817) 562-5351
(Supplier of machine-type batting by the yard; bulk orders only.)

————

Good Reference Books for Beginning Quilters

Quilts! Quilts! Quilts!!! The Complete Guide to Quiltmaking, by Diana McClun and Laura Nownes, Quilt Digest Press. (Everything you'll ever need to know about making a quilt, with projects.)

Patchwork Possibilities, by Marjorie Puckett, Orange Patchwork Publishers. (Wonderful step-by-step diagrams for basic quiltmaking in one inexpensive book.)

Template-Free Quiltmaking, More Template-Free Quiltmaking, Even More, Template-Free Quilts and Borders, all by Trudie Hughes, That Patchwork Place. (Each one of these books offers good basic directions for fast, rotary cutter, machine-made quilts, along with specific, recipe-style instructions for many projects.)

Heirloom Machine Quilting, by Harriet Hargrave, C&T Publishing. (Everything you need to know about machine quilting.)

About The Author

Jennifer Amor was born and educated in England, where fine hand sewing and polite conversation were almost as important for a young lady's upbringing as learning to ride and getting plenty of fresh air. As an aspiring twelve-year-old dress designer, she horrified the school matron with her first clothing project: a pink chiffon negligee, all stitched by hand! After frustrating attempts to sew grown-up suits on a toy chainstitch machine, she finally taught herself to make all her own clothes by machine as a teenager in Canada. A full-time quilter since 1979, she now concentrates on wearable art and bargello designs. Her quilts have won over 70 ribbons in regional, national and international shows. She teaches quiltmaking all over the United States and writes regularly for a number of quilting magazines.

⟨American Quilter's Society⟩
dedicated to publishing books for today's quilters

The following AQS publications are currently available:

• **American Beauties: Rose & Tulip Quilts**
by Gwen Marston & Joe Cunningham
#1907: AQS, 1988, 96 pages, softbound, $14.95

• **America's Pictorial Quilts** by Caron L. Mosey
#1662: AQS, 1985, 112 pages, hardbound, $19.95

• **Applique Designs: My Mother Taught Me to Sew**
by Faye Anderson
#2121: AQS, 1990, 80 pages, softbound, $12.95

• **Arkansas Quilts: Arkansas Warmth**
Arkansas Quilter's Guild, Inc.
#1908: AQS, 1987, 144 pages, hardbound, $24.95

• **The Art of Hand Applique** by Laura Lee Fritz
#2122: AQS, 1990, 80 pages, softbound, $14.95

• **...Ask Helen More About Quilting Designs** by Helen Squire
#2099: AQS, 1990, 54 pages, 17 x 11, spiral-bound, $14.95

• **Award-Winning Quilts & Their Makers:**
The Best of AQS Shows – 1985-1987 edited by Victoria Faoro
#2207: AQS, 1991, 232 pages, softbound, $19.95

• **Classic Basket Quilts** by Elizabeth Porter and Marianne Fons
#2208: AQS, 1991, 128 pages, softbound, $16.95

• **A Collection of Favorite Quilts** by Judy Florence
#2119 AQS, 1990, 136 pages, softbound, $18.95

• **Dear Helen, Can You Tell Me?**
...all about quilting designs by Helen Squire
#1820: AQS, 1987, 56 pages, 17 x 11, spiral-bound, $12.95

• **Dyeing & Overdyeing of Cotton Fabrics** by Judy Mercer Tescher
#2030: AQS, 1990, 54 pages, softbound, $9.95

• **Flavor Quilts for Kids to Make: Complete Instructions for Teaching Children To Dye, Decorate & Sew Quilts**
by Jennifer Amor
#2356, AQS, 1991, 120 pages., softbound, $12.95

• **Fun & Fancy Machine Quiltmaking** by Lois Smith
#1982: AQS, 1989, 144 pages, softbound, $19.95

• **Gallery of American Quilts: 1849-1988**
#1938: AQS, 1988, 128 pages, softbound, $19.95

• **Gallery of American Quilts 1860-1989: Book II**
#2129: AQS, 1990, 128 pages, softbound, $19.95

• **The Grand Finale: A Quilter's Guide to Finishing Projects**
by Linda Denner
#1924: AQS, 1988, 96 pages, softbound, $14.95

• **Heirloom Miniatures** by Tina M. Gravatt
#2097: AQS, 1990, 64 pages, softbound, $9.95

• **Home Study Course in Quiltmaking**
by Jeannie M. Spears
#2031: AQS, 1990, 240 pages, softbound, $19.95

• **Infinite Stars** by Gayle Bong
#2283: AQS, 1992, 72 pages, softbound, $12.95

• **The Ins and Outs: Perfecting the Quilting Stitch**
by Patricia J. Morris
#2120: AQS, 1990, 96 pages, softbound, $9.95

• **Irish Chain Quilts: A Workbook of Irish Chains & Related Patterns** by Joyce B. Peaden
#1906: AQS, 1988, 96 pages, softbound, $14.95

• **Marbling Fabrics for Quilts: A Guide for Learning & Teaching**
by Kathy Fawcett and Carol Shoaf
#2206: AQS, 1991, 72 pages, softbound, $12.95

• **Missouri Heritage Quilts** by Bettina Havig
#1718: AQS, 1986, 104 pages, softbound, $14.95

• **Nancy Crow: Quilts and Influences** by Nancy Crow
#1981: AQS, 1990, 256 pages, hardcover, $29.95

• **No Dragons on My Quilt** by Jean Ray Laury with
Ritva Laury and Lizabeth Laury
#2153: AQS, 1990, 52 pages, hardcover, $12.95

• **Oklahoma Heritage Quilts** Oklahoma Quilt Heritage Project
#2032: AQS, 1990, 144 pages, softbound, $19.95

• **Quiltmaker's Guide: Basics & Beyond** by Carol Doak
#2284: AQS, 1992, 208 pages, softbound $19.95

• **QUILTS: The Permanent Collection – MAQS**
#2257: AQS, 1991, 100 pages, 10 x 6½, softbound, $9.95

• **Scarlet Ribbons: American Indian Technique for Today's Quilters**
by Helen Kelley
#1819: AQS, 1987, 104 pages, softbound, $15.95

• **Sets & Borders** by Gwen Marston and Joe Cunningham
#1821: AQS, 1987, 104 pages, softbound, $14.95

• **Somewhere in Between: Quilts and Quilters of Illinois**
by Rita Barrow Barber
#1790: AQS, 1986, 78 pages, softbound, $14.95

• **Stenciled Quilts for Christmas** by Marie Monteith Sturmer
#2098: AQS, 1990, 104 pages, softbound, $14.95

• **Texas Quilts – Texas Treasures** Texas Heritage Quilt Society
#1760: AQS, 1986, 160 pages, hardbound, $24.95

• **A Treasury of Quilting Designs** by Linda Goodmon Emery
#2029: AQS, 1990, 80 pages, 14 x 11, spiral-bound, $14.95

• **Wonderful Wearables: A Celebration of Creative Clothing**
by Virginia Avery
#2286: AQS, 1991, 168 pages, softbound, $24.95

These books can be found in local bookstores and quilt shops. If you are unable to locate a title in your area, you can order by mail from AQS, P.O. Box 3290, Paducah, KY 42002-3290. Please add $1 for the first book and 40¢ for each additional one to cover postage and handling.